Practice Book

In the U.S.A.™

NATIONAL GEOGRAPHIC   **Hampton-Brown**

Acknowledgments and credits continue on the inside back cover.
The National Geographic Society John M. Fahey, Jr., President & Chief Executive Officer, Gilbert M. Grosvenor, Chairman of the Board
Copyright © 2011 The Hampton-Brown Company, Inc., a wholly owned subsidiary of the National Geographic Society, publishing under
the imprints National Geographic School Publishing and Hampton-Brown.

All rights reserved. No part of this book may be reproduced or transmitted in any form or by any means, electronic or mechanical,
including photocopying, recording, or by an information storage and retrieval system, without permission in writing from the Publisher.
National Geographic and the Yellow Border are registered trademarks of the National Geographic Society.

National Geographic School Publishing
Hampton-Brown
www.NGSP.com

Printed in the USA.
DB Hess, Woodstock, IL

ISBN: 978-0-7362-8010-5

18 19   11

Acknowledgments

Illustrations: Cover, Title Joel Soleto/Visual Asylum. **13** From Here to There by Marjorie Cuyler. Text copyright © 1999 by Margery Cuyler. Illustrations © 1999 by Yu Cha Pak. Used courtesy of Henry Holt and Company. **15** (tm, tr, bl-r) Darthouth Publishing, Inc. 23 Ben Shannon. **27-30** Terry Julien. **55** Ben Shannon. **61-64** Terry Julien. **89** Ben Shannon. **93-96** Terry Wong. **119** Darthmouth Publishing, Inc. **123** Ben Shannon. **127-130** Terry Julien. **133** Jun Park. **153, 157-160** Ben Shannon.

Photographs: 1 (bl) Ted Foxx/Alamy, (tl) BananaStock/Jupiterimages, (tr) BananaStock/Jupiterimages. **2** (bl) iStockphoto.com/JarekSzymanski, (ml) Kablonk!/Photolibrary, (tl) Michael Newman/PhotoEdit, (tr) Jack Hollingsworth/BigStockPhoto.com. **3** Row 1 (lml) PhotoDisc/Getty Images, (ml) Digital Stock, (mr) PhotoDisc/Getty Images, (r) Artville, (rmr) PhotoDisc/Getty Images, (l) Feng Yu/iStockphoto; Row 2 (l) Ryan McVay/Getty Images, (m) Digital Stock, (r) Metaphotos; Row 3 (l) LWA/Getty Images, (m) Harald Sund/Getty Images, (r) PhotoDisc/Getty Images; Row 4 (l) Steve Cole/Getty Images, (m) Paul Beard/Getty Images, (r) PhotoDisc/Getty Images. **4** Row 1 (m) PhotoDisc/Getty Images, (r) Paul Beard/Getty Images, (l) Feng Yu/iStockphoto; Row 2 (l) PhotoDisc/Getty Images, (m) EyeWire, (r) Digital Stock, Row 3 (l) PhotoDisc/Getty, Images, (m) Metaphotos, (r) PhotoDisc/Getty Images; Row 4 (l) Digital Stock, (m) Digital Stock, (r) PhotoDisc/Getty Images; Row 5 (l) Artville, (m) Steve Cole/Getty Images, (r) PhotoDisc/Getty Images. **5** Liz Gara Williams. **7** Row 1 (l) Artville, (r) Lancelot/Photononstop/Photolibrary.com; Row 2 (l) Ron Chapple Stock/Photolibrary.com, (r) Liz Garza Williams; Row 3 (l) Ron Chapple Stock/Photolibrary.com, (r) Getty Images; Row 4 (l) Getty Images, (m) Artville; Row 5 (l) Liz Garza Williams, (r) White Packert/Getty Images. **8** Row 1 (l) Ron Chapple Stock/Photolibrary.com, (r) Liz Garza Williams; Row 2 (l) Lancelot/Photononstop/Photolibrary.com, (r) Liz Garza Williams; Row 3 (l) Artville, (r) Liz Garza Williams; Row 4(l) Getty Images, (r) Liz Garza Williams; Row 5 (l) Getty Images, (r) White Packert/Getty Images. 10 (tl) Pixland/Jupiterimages. **15** (tl) Hill Street Studios/Blend Images/Corbis. **16** Row 1 (l) Brand X/Corbis, (m) John Paul Endress, (r) PhotoDisc/Getty Images; Row 2 (l) shinypix/Alamy, (m) PhotoDisc/Getty Images, (r) feng yu/BitStockPhoto.com. **17** (mr) Le Do/BigStockPhoto.com; (tr) Vladislav Ageshin/BigStockPhoto.com; Row 1 (l) PhotoDisc/Getty Images, (m) PhotoDisc/Getty Images, (r) MetaTools; Row 2 (l) feng yu/BitStockPhoto.com, (m) Image1/Photolibrary, (r) Getty Images. **18** (bl) Artville, (ml) Corbis/Jupiterimages, (mr) PhotoDisc/Getty Images. **21** Yellow Dog Productions/Jupiterimages. **22** (b) Ryan McVay/Jupiterimages, (m) Gunter Marx/Alamy, (t) Liz Garza Williams. **25** Row 1 (l) Dynamic Graphics/Creatas Images/Jupiterimages, (m) UpperCut Images/Alamy, (r) Marek Slusarczyk/BigStockPhoto.com; Row 2 (l) Masterfile, (m) Blend Images/Alamy, (r) David Young-Wolff/PhotoEdit. **26** (br) Image Club, (mr) Artville. **31** Image1/Photolibrary. **33** Row 1 (l) amridesign/Fotolia, (m) pkruger/BigStockPhoto.com, (r) Jupiterimages/Creatas/Alamy; Row 2 (l) Hank Shiffman/BigStockPhoto.com, (m) Jupiterimages/Creatas/Almay. (r) Jupiterimages/Creatas/Alamy. **34** (a) Gbh7/Dearamstime.com, (b) PhotoDisc/Getty Images, (c) pkruger/BigStockPhoto.com, (d) Jupiterimages/Creatas/Almay, (e) Richard Lewisohn/Getty Images. **35** Row 1 (l) PhotoDisc/Getty Images, (lml) Janis Christie/Getty Images, (m, r) Artville, (rmr) Liz Garza Williams; Row 2 (l) SuperStock, (m) John Paul Endress, (r) Getty Images; Row 3 (l) PhotoDisc/Getty Images, (m) Artville, (r) Liz Garza Williams; Row 4 (l) Digital Stock, (m) PhotoDisc/Getty Images, (r) PhotoDisc/Getty Images; Row 5 (l) MetaTools, (m) John Paul Endress, (r) Liz Garza Williams. **36** Row 1 (l) Artville, (m) D. Falconer/PhotoLink/Getty Images, (r) PhotoDisc/Getty Images; Row 2 (l) Ron Chapple Stock/Photolibrary.com, (m) Stockbyte/Getty Images, (r) Liz Garza Williams; Row 3 (l) PhotoDisc/Getty Images, (m) Getty Images, (r) Liz Garza Williams; Row 4 (l) Liz Garza Williams, (m) Getty Images, (r) PhotoDisc/Getty Images. **39** Row 1(l) Liz Garza Williams, (r) D. Falconer/PhotoLink/Getty Images; Row 2 (l) Liz Garza Williams, (r) White Packert/Getty Images; Row 3 (l) Getty Images, (r) PhotoDisc/Getty Images; Row 4 (ml mr) PhotoDisc/Getty Images, (r) D. Falconer/PhotoLink/Getty Images; Row 5 (l) Artville, (mlm mr) Liz Garza Williams, (r) White Packert/Getty Images. **40** Row 1 (l) Artville, (r) Getty Images; Row 2 (l) Ron Chapple Stock/Photolibrary.com, (r) PhotoDisc/Getty Images; Row 3 (l) Liz Garza Williams, (r) D. Falconer/PhotoLink/Getty Images; Row 4 (l) Paul Beard/Getty Images, (ml) D. Falconer/PhotoLink/Getty Images, (mr, r) Liz Garza Williams; Row 5 (l) Digital Stock, (ml) Getty Images, (r) Liz Garza Williams; Row 6 (l) Liz Garza Williams, (ml) PhotoDisc/Getty Images, (mr) Stockbyte/Getty Images, (r) Liz Garza Williams. **42** (l) David Young-Wolff/PhotoEdit, (ml) Itani/Alamy, (mr) Custom Medical Stock Photo/Alamy, (r) lisafx/BigStockPhoto.com. **43** (a) Jupiterimages, (b, c) PhotoDisc/Getty Images, (d) Artville. **46** Getty Images. **52** (bl) Will & Deni McIntyre/CORBIS, (br) Lon C. Diehl/PhotoEdit, (ml) robophobic/BigStockPhoto.com, (mr) Blend Images/Alamy, (tl) moodboard/corbis, (tr) Masterfile. **53** (bl) Corbis RF/Alamy, (br) Juniors Bildarchiv/Alamy, (tl) Masterfile, (tr) Al Fuchs/NewSport/Corbis. **54** (a) Blend Images, (b) Corbis, (c) Richard Lewisohn/Getty Images, (d) PhotoDisc/Getty Images. **57** (1) David Buffington/Jupiterimages, (1r) BananaStock/Jupiterimages, (2) Tom & Dee Ann McCarthy/Corbis, (2r) Getty Images, (3) Simon Jarratt/Corbis, (3r) Michael Newman/PhotoEdit, (4) Yellow Dog Productions/Jupiterimages, (5) sozaijiten/Datacraft/Getty Images, (6) Jupiterimages, (6r) iStockphoto.com/JarekSzymanski, (7) Aflo Sport/Masterfile, (8) Jupiterimages. (8r) Jack Hollingsworth/BigStockPhoto.com. **58** (bg) Jim Lane/Alamy, (br) Creatas/PhotoLibrary, (tl) Images-USA/Alamy, (tr) Brand X Pictures/Photolibrary. **59** (bl) Stuart Cohen/The Image Works, (br) LatinStock Collection/Alamy, (ml) Danita Delimont/Alamy, (mr) PhotoDisc/Getty Images, (tl) Masterfile, (tr) Janine Wiedel Photolibrary/Alamy. **60** (mr) PhotoDisc/Getty Images, (tr) Richard Lewisohn/Getty Images. **65** Copyright © 1999 by Shaki for Children. Used with permission by Charlesbridge Publishing, Inc. All rights reserved. **67** (bl, br) NGSP, (ml, mr, tr) Artville, (tl) C Squared Studios/PhotoDisc/Getty Images. **68** (b) Ingram Publishing/Superstock, (m, r) PhotoDisc/Getty Images. **69** Row 1 (r) Rena Schild/Shutterstock, (l) Getty Images, (lml) Brian Klutch/Digital Vision, (m) PhotoDisc/Getty Images, (rmr) Artville; Row 2 (l) SuperStock, Inc./SuperStock, (ml) Corbis, (mr) Ryan McVay/Getty Images, (r) Alex Slobodkin/iStockphotos.com; Row 3 (l, ml) Artville, (mr) Getty Images, (r) John Paul Endress; Row 4 (l, mr) John Paul Endress, (ml) Getty Images, (r) Jack Fields/CORBIS; Row 5 (l, r) Artville, (ml) Getty Images, (mr) EyeWire. **70** (l) John Paul Endress, (m) Artville, (r) Liz Garza Williams; Row 2 (l) PhotoDisc/Getty Images, (m, r) Getty Images; Row 3 (l) Laura Dwight/CORBIS, (m) Liz Garza Williams, (r) D. Falconer/PhotoLink/Getty Images; Row 4 (l, r) PhotoDisc/Getty Images, (m) Getty Images. **71** Row 1 (l) PhotoDisc/Getty Images, (m) Jupiterimages, (r) Metatools; Row 2 (l) Steven von Niederhausern/iStockphoto.com, (m) Artville, (r) jerryhat/iStockphoto.com; Row 3 (l) PhotoDisc/Getty Images, (m) Artville, (r) Stockbyte/Getty Images; Row 4 (l) Stockbyte/Getty Images, (m) jerryhat/iStockphoto.com, (r) bedo/iStockphoto.com; Row 5 (l) Metatools, (m) Klaudia Stiener/iStockphoto.com, (r) MetaTools. **72** (bl) Image Source/Corbis, (br) Brand X Pictures/Getty Images, (ml) Artville, (mr) David Young-Wolff/PhotoEdit, (tl) PhotoDisc/Getty Images, (tr) Artville. **73** (ml, mr, tr, tl) Liz Garza Williams. **74** Row 1 (l) Liz Garza Williams, (m) Getty Images, (r) Laura Dwight/CORBIS; Row 2 (l) Getty Images, (m) PhotoDisc/Getty Images, (r) John Paul Endress; Row 3 (l) White Packert/Getty Images, (m) D. Falconer/PhotoLink/Getty Images, (r) PhotoDisc/Getty Images; Row 4 (l) Artville, (m) Thom Lang/Corbis; Row 5 (l) Getty Images, (m) PhotoDisc/Getty Images, (r) Liz Garza Williams. **75** Row 1 (l) Bill Aron/PhotoEdit, (m) PhotoDisc/Getty Images, (r) Liz Garza Williams; Row 2 (m) Getty Images, (r) C Square Studios/Getty Images; Row 3 (l) Laura Dwight/CORBIS, (m, r) Artville; Row 4 (l) Laura Dwight/CORBIS, (ml) PhotoDisc/Getty Images, (mr) White Packert/Getty Images, (r) PhotoDisc/Getty Images; Row 5 (l) D. Falconer/PhotoLink/Getty Images, (ml) Ryan McVay/Getty Images; Row 6 (l) Getty Images, (ml) PhotoDisc/Getty Images, (mr) C Square Studios/Getty Images, (r) Stockbyte/Getty Images. **76** Row 1 (l) dmac/Alamy, (r) Artville; Row 2 (l) Ilene MacDonald/Alamy, (r) Artville; Row 3 (l, r) Artville; Row 4 (lb) Ilene MacDonald/Alamy, (lc) dmac/Alamy, (lr) Artville, (m) Corbis, (r) Artville; Row 5 (l) Visions of America, LLC/Alamy, (m) Artville. **77** (bl) Juanmonino/iStockphoto.com, (br) PhotoDisc/Getty Images, (ml) Brand X Pictures/Getty Images, (mr) David Young-Wolff/PhotoEdit, (tl) Matej Michelizza/iStockphoto.com, (tr) Steven von Niederhausern/iStockphoto.com. **78** (a) Trinacria Photo/Shutterstock, (b) Sylvain Grandadam/photolibrary.com, (c, d) PhotoDisc/Getty Images. **81** (l) Image Source/Fotosearch, (r)Lindsay Edwards. **83** (bl) Tan Wei Ming/Dreamstime.com, (br) Picturelake/Dreamstime.com, (ml) Bill Aron/PhotoEdit, (mr) epantha/Fotolia, (tr) Luminis/Alamy. **87** (bl) JUPITERIMAGES/Brand X/Alamy, (ml) Digital Vision Ltd./SuperStock, (mr) Elvele Images Ltd/Alamy, (r) Kevin Britland/BigtockPhoto.com, (tl) Jupiterimages, (tr) zefa/Corbis/Jupiterimages. **88** (b) Kadroff/Shutterstock, (m) Apollofoto/Dreamstime.com, (t) Image Club. **91** (l) josunshine/Fotolia, (lml) Dana Bartekoske/BigStockPhoto.com, (m) Ed Brennan/Fotolia, (r) Andrew Johnson/iStockphoto, (rmr) Sue Smith/BigStockPhoto.com. **97** Liz Garza Williams. **99** Stockbyte/Getty Images. **100** Christopher Futcher/Shutterstock. **101** (bl) Jason Stitt/Fotolia, (br) BananaStock/Jupiterimges, (ml) Rob/Fotolia, (mr) Philip Date/Fotolia, (tl) JOE GIZA/Reuters/Corbis, (tr) Rosmizan Abu seman/BigStockPhoto.com. **102** (b) Polka Dot Images/Jupiterimages, (m) PhotoDisc/Getty Images, (t) Funkipics/Dreamstime/com.

103 (l) Premier Edition Image Library/Superstock, (lm Stockbyte/Getty Images, (m) Gavin Heiller/Getty Imag Digital Studio, (rmr) PhotoDisc/Getty Images, (r) Brian Klutch/Digital Vision. **104** Row 1 (l) Laura Dwight/CO (m) John Paul Endress, (r) Liz Garza Williams; Row 2 (l) Garza Williams, (m) John Paul Endress, (r) Getty Image 3 (l) Getty Images, (m) Artville, (r) Charles Krebs/Getty Images; Row 4 (l) Digital Studio, (m) Duomo/CORBIS, (Klutch/Digital Vision. **105** (bl) JodiJacobson/iStockph (br) Ian Boddy/Science Photo Library/Photolibrary, (tl) Stitt/Fotolia, (tr) Ronald Sumners/Shutterstock. **107** R (l) C Square Studios/Getty Images, (ml, mr) Liz Garza Williams, (r) David Young-Wolff/PhotoEdit; Row 2 (l, m Artville, (r) Getty Images; Row 3 (l) John Paul Endress, PhotoDisc/Getty Images, (r) Getty Images; Row 4 (l, m Garza Williams, (mr) Artville, (r) David Young-Wolff/PhotoEdit; Row 5 (m, r) Liz Garza Williams; Row 6 (l) D. Falconer/PhotoLink/Getty Images, (m) Ryan McVay/G Images, (r) Laura Dwight/CORBIS. **108** Row 1 (l, ml) Liz Williams, (mr) Getty Images, (r) PhotoDisc/Getty Imag Row 2 (l) Getty Images, (m) Bill Aron/PhotoEdit, (r) D. Falconer/PhotoLink/Getty Images; Row 3 (l) PhotoDisc Getty Images, (m) Laura Dwight/CORBIS, (r) Liz Garza Williams; Row 4 (l, m) Getty Images, (r) Duomo/CORBIS 5 (l) Charles Krebs/Getty Images, (m) John Paul Endres Liz Garza Williams; Row 6 (l) David Young-Wolff/Photo (m) Getty Imgaes, (r) Artville. **109** (bl) Elenathewise/Dreamstime, (br) DigitalStock/Corbis, (ml) Image Sour Jupiterimages, (mr) Jupiterimages, (tl) Steve Skjold/Al (tr) PhotoDisc/Getty Images. **110** (b) Jupiterimages, (r PhotoDisc/Getty Images, (t) PhotoDisc/Getty Images. **113** Photolibrary. **115** (bl) Catherine Antonin/iStockph (bm) jblah/Fotolia, (br) Izaokas Sapiro/Fotolis, (ml) Igo Terekhov/BigStockPhoto.com, (mr) photo25th/Fotolia (mrm) Leonid Nyshko/BigStockPhoto.com, (tl) Yury Maryunin/Fotolia, (tm) Flab/Alamy, (tr) SemA/Fotolia. **119** (b,m, tl, tm) Stockbyte/Getty Images. **120** (bl) Westend61 GmbH/Alamy, (br) Streetfly Stock/Alamy, (Jan Sandvik/BigStockPhoto.com, (mr) Nikreates/Alamy dniser/Fotolia, (tr) Smalik/Fotolia. **121** Scott B. Rosen. **122** (b) iofoto/Shutterstock, (m) Dimitriy Shironosov/Shutterstock, (t) Corbis. **125** (bl) Polka Dot Images/Jupiterimages, (br) Jordano/Dreamstime.com, (ml) An Johnson/iStockphoto, (mr) Jarenwicklund/Dreamstim com, (tl) Courtesy of Cheryle D'Amelio, (tr) Andrey Sha iStockphoto. **134** (b) Cherylcasey/Dreamstime.com, (r Sonya Etchison/Shutterstock, (t) PhotoDisc/Getty Ima **135** (l) John Paul Endress, (m, ml) Getty Images, (mr) A (r) Image Club. **136** Row 1 (r) Image Club, (l, m) PhotoD Getty Images; Row 2 (l) Roger Ressmeyer/Corbis, (m) Li Garza Williams; Row 3 (l) Siede Preis/Getty Images, (m) Garza Williams, (r) Eyewire; Row 4 (l) John Paul Endress Liz Garza Williams. **137** (bl) Lean-Luc Morales/Alamy, (PhotoDisc/Getty Images, (tl) Stephen Coburn/BigStockPhoto.com, (tr) Tim Hall/cultura/Jupiterimage **139** Row 1 (l) Getty Images, (m) PhotoDisc/Getty Imag Image Club; Row 2 (l) Ryan McVay/Getty Images, (m) Li Garza Williams, (r) Siede Preis/Getty Images; Row 3 (l) E Aron/PhotoEdit; Row 4 (l) Liz Gara Williams, (m) Roger Ressmeyer/Corbis, (r) PhotoDisc/Getty Images; Row 5 Garza Williams, (m) PhotoDisc/Getty Images, (r) D. Falc PhotoLink/Getty Images. **140** Row 1 (m) Bill Aron/PhotoEdit, (r) Getty Images; Row 2 (l) PhotoDisc/Getty Images, (m, r) Getty Images; Row 3 (l, r) PhotoDisc/Get Images, (m) Getty Images; Row 4 (l) Liz Garza Williams, PhotoDisc/Getty Images, (mr) Roger Ressmeyer/Corbis Artville; Row 5 (l, m) Liz Garza Williams, (r) Siede Preis/ Images; Row 6 (l) Liz Garza Williams, (ml) Paul Beard/G Images, (mr) Image Club, (r) Getty Images. **141** (bl) De MacDonald/Alamy, (br)Photos.com/Jupiterimages, (ml, Darrin Klimek/Getty Images, (tl) Jeff Greenberg/Alamy, Verity Smith/Brand X Pictures/Jupiterimages, (mr) Paul Glendell/Alamy. **142** (b) Gelpi/Shutterstock, (m) muzsy Shutterstock, (t) Monkey Business Images/Shutterstoc **145** Illustrations from Get Around in the City by Lee Su Hill. Copyright © by Lee Sullivan Hill. Used by permissi Carolrhoda Books, Inc., a division of Lerner Publishing Group. All rights reserved. **147** (bl) George Doyle/Gett Images, (br) GlowImages/Alamy, (ml) Maridav/Fotolia, Peter Griffith/Masterfile, (tl) Design Pics Inc./Alamy, (tr) Cathy Yeulet/BigStockPhoto.com. **151** (bl) MIXA Co. Li Photolibrary, (br) Keith Dannemiller/Corbis, (ml) Digita Vision/Alamy, (mr) Natalia Bratslavsky/iStockphoto, (tl) Hu/BigStockPhoto.com, (tr) Ryan McVay/PhotoDisc/Ge Images. **152** (b) Rob Friedman/iStockphoto, (m) Corbis Zvonimir/iStockphoto. **155** (tl) Sparkmom/Dreamstim com, (tr) Radius Images/Alamy, (ml) Jupiterimages/Get Images, (mr) David Kelly Crow/PhotoEdit, (bl) JGI/Blend Images/Jupiterimages, (br) Myrleen Ferguson Cate/PhotoEdit. **161** Alan Schein/Corbis.

Name _____

Give Personal Information

 Look at the names, addresses, and phone numbers. Draw or paste your picture to number 4. 🗨 Say the words that finish each sentence. ✍ Then write the words.

1.

Denis
155 Main Street
520-555-3147

Hi. My name is ____Denis____. I live at

____155 Main Street____. My phone

number is ____520-555-3147____.

3.

Khalid
12 River Road
214-555-6004

Hello. My name is _____. I live at

_____. My phone

number is _____.

2.

Luisa
5827 Main Street
520-555-2681

Hi. My name _____

_____. I ____live____

at ____5827 Main Street____.

My phone number _____

_____.

4.

_____. My _____ ____

_____. I _____

____ - _____.

My _____ _____ _____

_____.

Name_____

High Frequency Words

A. 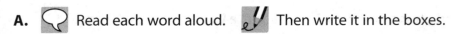 Read each word aloud. Then write it in the boxes.

1. **n a m e**
   ☐☐☐☐

2. **My** _____My_____ _____name_____ is _____Sam_____.

Sam

3. **a m** I _____am_____ _____Sam_____.

B. Write the missing words.

4.
   Pam

   _____ _____ is _____.

5.
   Matt

   _____ _____ is _____.

6.
   Tam

   I _____ _____.

© NGSP & H

Name _____

Letters and Sounds

A. Study the new letters and sounds.

| **Ss** | **Mm** | **Ff** | **Hh** | **Tt** | **Aa** |

B. Listen to each word. What letter spells the <u>first</u> sound you hear? Circle the letter.

1.

t   ⓗ   a

2.

a   h   s

3.

h   f   s

4.

f   h   a

5.

a   m   s

6.

t   h   a

7.

a   m   t

8.

a   s   m

9.

t   h   a

Name _____

Letters and Sounds

 Say the name of each picture below. What letter spells the <u>first</u> sound you hear? Write the letter.

1.

s
_____

2.

_____

3.

_____

4.

_____

5.

_____

6.

_____

7.

_____

8.

_____

9.

_____

10.

_____

11.

_____

12.

_____

13.

_____

14.

_____

15.

_____

© NGSP & H

Make Introductions

 Read the speech balloons below. What does each person say?
Write the words in each speech balloon.

| Nice to meet you. | Hello, Mrs. Walker. This is my friend Carlos. | Welcome, Carlos. Glad to meet you, too. | Carlos, this is Mrs. Walker. |

1.

2.

3.

4.

High Frequency Words

A. 🗨 Read each word aloud.   ✍ Then write it.

1. am _____   **4.** my _____

2. I _____   **5.** name _____

3. is _____   **6.** you _____

B.   **How to Play**

1. Make a spinner.

2. Spin.

3. Complete each sentence.
The first player to complete all
six sentences wins.

I _____ Sam.

My name
_____ Matt.

See _____ later!

_____ am at school.

This is
_____ school.

What is
your _____?

   © NGSP & H

Name _____

Words with Short *a*

A. Read each word.  Draw a line to match the word and the picture.

1.

hat

ham

2.

fat

mat

B.  Write the missing words.

3.

This is a ___hat___.
(ham / hat)

6.

I _____ Ron.
(Sam / am)

4.

Maylin is _____ school.
(at / sat)

7.

This is a _____.
(ham / hat)

5.

Here is the _____.
(fat / mat)

8.

You _____ at the 🪑.
(at / sat)

Words with Short *a*

A.  Write the missing *a*. 💬 Then read the words in each list. How are the words different?

1. _a_ m

     S ___ m

     h ___ m

2. ___ t

     h ___ t

     s ___ t

3. ___ t

     f ___ t

     m ___ t

B. What word completes each sentence and tells about the picture?

 Spell the word.

4.
 Here is my __h_ _a_ _t_.

5.
I am ___ ___ ___.

6.
This is a ___ ___ ___.

7.
I am ___ ___ school.

8.
 I ___ ___ Ron.

9.
 I ___ ___ ___ on the  .

10.
Sam ___ ___ ___ a [   ] .

11.
Look at the ___ ___ ___.

12.
I ___ ___ at the [   ] .

13.
 You ___ ___ ___ at the  .

  © NGSP & H

Name _____

Give Information

 Look at each picture.   Say the words that finish each sentence.

 Then write the words.

1.

I am from _____Russia_____.

Now I live in ___New York___.

2.

I am from _____.

Now I live in _____.

3.

I ___am___ _____.

_____.

Now I _____ _____

_____.

4.

I _____ _____

_____.

Now I _____ _____

_____.

5.
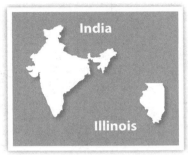

I'm from _____.

_____ _____ _____

_____ _____.

6.
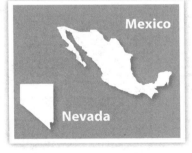

_____ _____

_____.

_____ _____ _____

_____ _____.

Name_____

High Frequency Words

A. 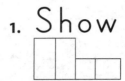 Read each word aloud. ✏ Then write it in the boxes.

1. Show
   ▢▢▢▢

2. me   _____Show_____ ___me___ your family.
   ▢▢

3. Look   _____Look_____ at my uncle.
   ▢▢▢▢

B. ✏ Write the missing words.

Russia

4. _____ me Russia.

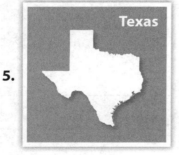
Texas

5. _____ at _____.

Mexico

6. Show _____ _____.

© NGSP & H

Write Words

A. 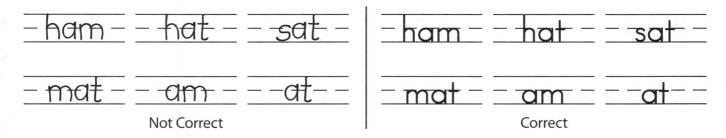 Look at the words.

ham hat sat	ham hat sat
mat am at	mat am at
Not Correct	Correct

B. Trace each word. Then write it.

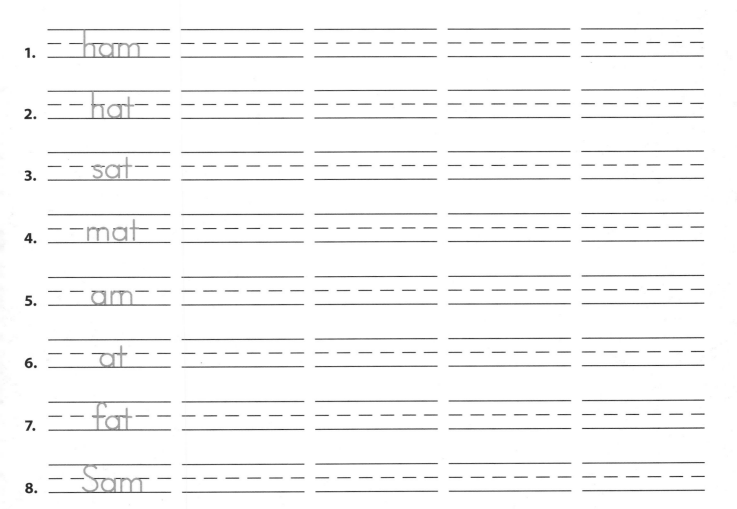

1. ham

2. hat

3. sat

4. mat

5. am

6. at

7. fat

8. Sam

Write Words

A. 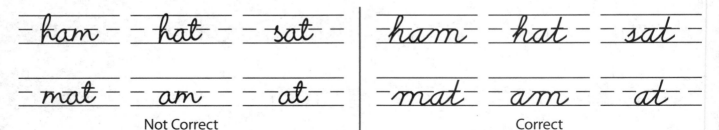 Look at the words.

ham	hat	sat
mat	am	at
Not Correct		

ham	hat	sat
mat	am	at
Correct		

B. Trace each word. Then write it.

1. ham

2. hat

3. sat

4. mat

5. am

6. at

7. fat

8. Sam

© NGSP & H

Reread and Retell

Write a place in each circle of the diagram to show where Maria lives.
Start with the smallest place.

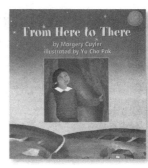

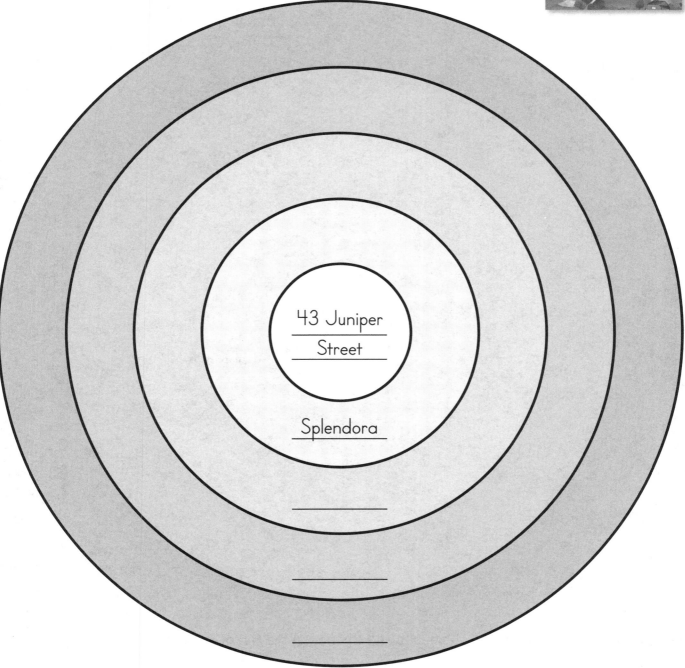

43 Juniper
Street

Splendora

_____

_____

_____

Write About Yourself

A.  Write about yourself. Draw pictures or tape some photos of yourself to this page.

Hi. I am

I am from

Now I live in

At home in

At home in

B. Check the writing. Do you need to add a period to the end of a sentence?

Do you need to add any capital letters?

© NGSP & H

Name _____

Give Information

 Look at each picture.   ✍ Color items 2–6. Use different colors.

💬 Say the words that finish each sentence.   ✍ Then write the words.

1.

This is a ____book____.

It is ____little____.

3.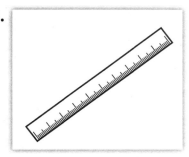

Here is ____ _____.

It is _____.

5.

I have ____ _____.

It ____ _____.

2.

This is __a__ _____.

It ____ _____.

4.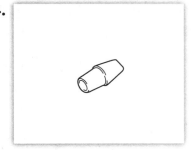

Here ____ ____ _____.

_____ _____.

_____.

6.

I _____ ____

_____. It

__ _____.

Name_____

Ask and Answer Questions

A. Look at each picture. 💬 Say the words that finish each question and answer.
Then write the words.

1.

___Is___ this a calculator?

Yes, it is.

3.

___ _____ ___ notebook?

No, _____ _____ _____.

It's a _____.

5.

___ _____ ____ eraser?

_____ , _____ _____.

2.

_____ _____ a ruler?

No, it is not. It's a ___pen___.

4.

____ _____ ____ pen?

No, ____ isn't.

It's ____ _____.

6.

____ _____ ____ pair

of scissors?

No, _____ _____.

B. Draw a school tool. Write a question for it that is not true.
Then answer the question with the true answer.

_____ _____ _____ _____?

_____ , _____ _____.

_____ _____ _____.

© NGSP & H

Name _____

High Frequency Words

A. Read each word aloud.  Then write it in the boxes.

1. Point

Point to the pen.

2. the

3. This   This is a ruler.

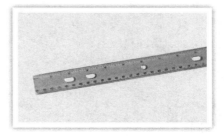

B. Write the missing words.

4.

_____ is an eraser.

5.

_____ to _____
notebook.

6.

_____ is a
_____.

7.

_____ to _____
_____.

8.

_____ is ____
_____.

9.

_____ to _____
_____.

Name_____

High Frequency Words

A. 🗨 Read each word aloud.   ✍ Then write it.

1. this _____   4. point _____

2. the _____   5. look _____

3. me _____   6. show _____

B. **7.** Find the words. Circle them.
Look across. ➡

q	t	h	i	s	m
v	k	e	s	l	w
s	b	t	t	h	e
t	l	j	q	t	q
z	p	r	g	m	e
l	o	o	k	q	o
w	f	s	h	o	w
p	o	i	n	t	r

8. Find the words. Circle them.
Look down. ⬇

m	q	t	j	z	t
e	v	h	u	l	s
k	s	i	r	o	g
o	h	s	p	o	t
r	o	i	o	k	h
x	w	y	i	r	e
w	g	o	n	z	q
p	u	z	t	a	v

C. ✍ Write the missing words.

9. _____ me Mexico.
   (Show / This)

10. _____ is a pen. ✒
   (This / Me)

11. Can you help _____?
   (the / me)

12. _____ at the book.
   (Look / This)

✍ Write the missing words.

13. _____ to the
   (Me / Point)
   of the United States.

14. _____ teacher is
   (Show / The)
   from ⬦ .

                    © NGSP & ⊦

Write Sentences

A. Look at the statements.

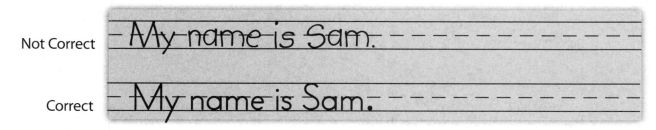

Not Correct — My name is Sam.

Correct — My name is Sam.

B. Trace each sentence. Then write it.

1. My name is Matt.

2. I am Sam.

3. I am Matt.

4. Sam sat.

5. Matt sat.

6. Show me Sam.

7. Show me Matt.

8. Show me a map.

Name_____

Write Sentences

A. Look at the statements.

Not Correct

My name is Sam.

Correct

My name is Sam.

B. Trace each sentence. Then write it.

1. *My name is Matt.* _____

2. *I am Sam.* _____

3. *I am Matt.* _____

4. *Sam sat.* _____

5. *Matt sat.* _____

6. *Show me Sam.* _____

7. *Show me Matt.* _____

8. *Show me a map.* _____

© NGSP &

Give and Follow Commands

 Say each command. Your partner points to the object in the picture.

1. Point to a map.

2. Show me a circle.

3. Show me a chair.

4. Point to a desk.

5. Point to a rectangle.

6. Point to the teacher.

7. Show me a student.

8. Show me a book.

9. Show me the board.

High Frequency Words

A. 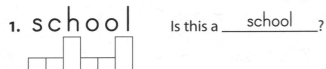 Read each word aloud. Then write it in the boxes.

1. s c h o o l   Is this a ____school____?

2. Y e s   ____Yes____, it is a school.

3. I t   ____It____ is big.

B. Write the missing words.

4. Is this a _____?

5. _____, _____ is a _____.

6. _____ is small.

7. Is this a _____?

8. _____, _____ is a _____.

 © NGSP &

Tam is at school.

The Hats

This is Tam.

Tam has a hat.

Mat, no hats in school!

Illustrated by Ben Shannon © NGSP & HB

Hi. I am Mat.

Look at *my* hat, Tam!

Mat has a hat.

(title)

Name _____

Ask and Answer Questions

 Look at each picture. Say the words that finish each question and answer.

Then write the words.

1.

What is in the ___bathroom___?

A ___sink___ is ___in___ the

bathroom.

2.

What is ___on___ the ___tray___?

A _____ is on

the _____.

3.

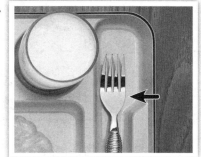

What is _____ the _____?

A _____ is on

the _____.

4.

What is _____ the wall?

A _____ is _____ the

_____.

5.

What is _____

the _____?

A _____ is

_____ the _____.

6.

What is ___ the classroom?

A _____ is _____

the _____.

Name _____

High Frequency Words

A. 🗨 Read each word aloud. ✍ Then write it.

1. number _____   4. not _____

2. it _____   5. school _____

3. no _____   6. yes _____

B. ✍ Write the letters.

    7. Which words have a **t**?

        n   o   t

        ___ ___ ___

    8. Which words have 2 letters?

        ___ ___

        ___ ___

    9. Which words have 3 letters?

        ___ ___ ___

        ___ ___ ___

    10. Which word ends with **r**?

        ___ ___ ___ ___ ___ ___

    11. Which word starts with **s**?

        ___ ___ ___ ___ ___ ___

    12. Which words start with **n**?

        ___ ___ ___ ___ ___ ___

        ___ ___ ___

        ___ ___ ___

C. ✍ Write the missing word.

13. This is my ___school___.
            (school / not)

14. _____ is a small school.
    (No / It)

15. My desk is in room _____ 5.
                  (number / yes)

16. It is _____ big.
      (school / not)

17. Is this a pen?

    _____ , it is a pen.
    (Yes / No)

18. Is this a book?

    _____ , this is not a book.
    (Yes / No)

© NGSP &

This Is Tam

© NGSP & HB

Tam is fast!

This is Tam.

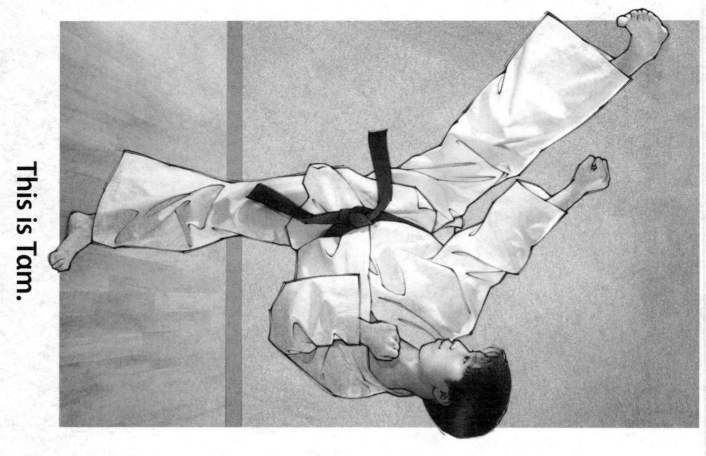

© NGSP & HB

Look at Tam!

This is the school.

© NGSP & HB

This is the mat.

Tam is at school.

© NGSP & HB

Show me the mat.

Tam has a mat.

Reread and Retell

Write a shape in each oval of the diagram. For each shape, write the names of things that are that shape.

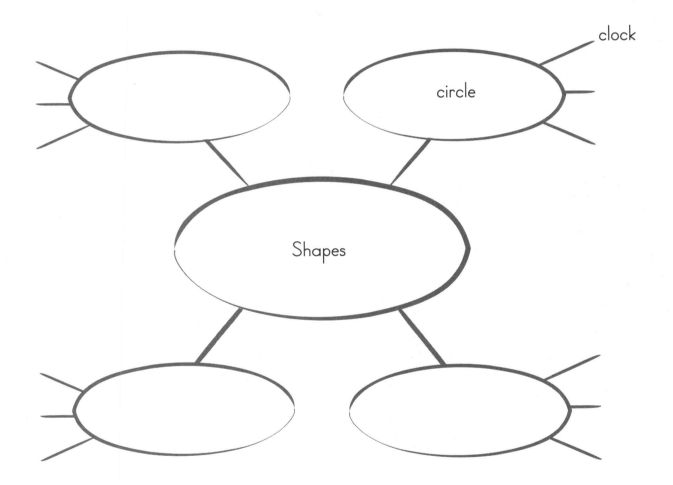

clock

circle

Shapes

Write About Your Schools

A.  Write about your schools. Draw pictures or tape some photos of your schools to this page.

Here is

My school in

Here is my school in

My school in

B. Check the writing. Do you need to add a capital letter for the first word of a sentence?

Do you need to add capital letters for the names of cities, states, or countries?

  © NGSP & H

Name _____

Ask and Answer Questions

 Look at each picture.   Say the words that finish each question and answer. Then write the words.

1.

What time is it?

___It___ ___is___ 5:15.

2.

What time ____ ____?

It ____ _____.

3.

What _____ ____ ____?

____ ____ _____.

4.

What day is it?

____ ____ Tuesday.

5.

What day ____ ____?

It ____ _____.

6.

_____ ____ ____ ____?

____ ____ _____.

Name _____

High Frequency Words

A. 💬 Read each word aloud. ✍️ Then write it in the boxes.

1. t i m e   What __time__ is it?

2. a t   School starts __at__ 8:30 every __day__.

3. d a y

B. ✍️ Write the missing words.

4. What _____ is lunch?

5. Lunch is _____ 11:00.

6. What _____ is it?

7. What _____ is P.E.?

8. P.E. is _____ 10:30 every _____.

     © NGSP &

Name _____

Letters and Sounds

A.  Study the new letters and sounds.

                   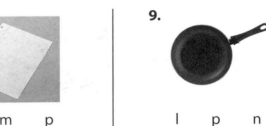

Nn   **Ll**   **Pp**   **Gg**   **Ii**

B.  Listen to each word. What letter spells the <u>first</u> sound you hear?  Circle the letter.

1.

   (n)   f   a

2.

   l   p   n

3.

   s   l   n

4.

   t   h   i

5.

   f   m   p

6.

   g   p   l

7.

   p   f   i

8.

   l   n   t

9.

   l   p   n

10.

   l   g   n

11.

   t   g   a

12.

   l   g   f

Name_____

Letters and Sounds

 Say the name of each picture below. What letter spells the <u>first</u> sound you hear? Write the letter.

1.

_____ h _____

2.

_____

3.

_____

4.

_____

5.

_____

6.

_____

7.

_____

8.

_____

9.

_____

10.

_____

11.

_____

12.

_____

© NGSP & H

Ask and Answer Questions

Look at the plan for Mr. Smith's class. Say the words that finish each question and answer. Then write the words.

Mr. Smith's Class Plan		
Science	9:30	Room 5
Lunch	11:30	Lunch Room
ESL Class	1:00	Room 124
P.E.	2:00	Gym

1. Where is P.E.?

It's in the _____gym_____.

2. When is science?

It's ____at____ ____9:30____.

3. Where is ____lunch____?

It's in the lunch room.

4. When is lunch?

It's _____ _____.

5. Where is _____?

It's _____ Room 5.

6. Where _____ ESL?

_____ _____ Room 124.

High Frequency Words

A. 🗨 Read each word aloud.   ✍ Then write it.

1. at	_____	**4.** time	_____
2. day	_____	**5.** what	_____
3. tomorrow	_____	**6.** who	_____

B. ✍ Write the letters.

7. Which words have 4 letters?

t i m e
___ ___ ___ ___

w h a t
___ ___ ___ ___

8. Which words have an **o**?

___ ___ ___

___ ___ ___ ___ ___ ___ ___ ___

9. Which word has 2 letters?

___ ___

10. Which words have 3 letters?

___ ___ ___

___ ___ ___

11. Which words have an **a**?

___ ___ ___

___ ___ ___

___ ___ ___ ___

12. Which words have an **h**?

___ ___ ___

___ ___ ___ ___

C. ✍ Write the missing word.

13. What _____time_____ is
            (time / who)
math class?

14. I have math class
_____ 10:30.
            (day / at)

15. _____ time is it?
            (Who / What)

16. What _____ do you
            (at / day)
have P.E.?

17. I have it _____.
            (day / tomorrow)

18. _____ is
            (Who / Time)
your teacher?

   © NGSP &

Name _____

Words with Short *a* and *i*

A. Read each word. Draw a line to match the word and the picture.

1.

pan

map

man

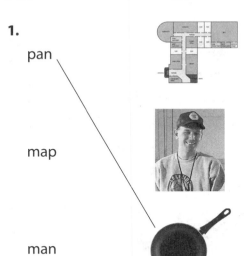

2.

pin

sit

pig

B. Write the missing words.

3.

She has a
___hat___.

(mat / hat)

5.

This is a
_____.

(fan / man)

7.

This is a
_____.

(pin / pig)

9.

This is a
_____.

(pan / pig)

4.

This is a
_____.

(pan / ham)

6.

_____ it!

(Pin / Hit)

8.

He is a
_____.

(man / mat)

10.

You
_____

(sit / hit)

in a .

Name_____

Words with Short *a* and *i*

A. Write the missing letters. Then read the words in each list. How are the words different?

1.

h __ __ __

___ ___ ___

___ ___ ___

2.
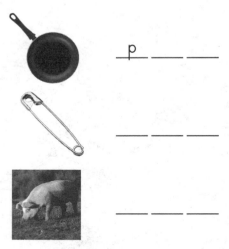
p __ __ __

___ ___ ___

___ ___ ___

B. Read each question. What word goes in the answer? Write the word.

Then circle the correct picture.

3. Where is the pig?

The __p__ __i__ __g__ is here.

4. Where is the pan?

Here is the ____ ____ ____.

5. Where is Sam?

Here is ____ ____ ____.

6. Who hit it?

Carlos ____ ____ ____ it.

7. Who has the hat?

She ____ ____ ____ the hat.

8. Who is the man?

He is the ____ ____ ____.

© NGSP & H

Ask and Answer Questions

Look at the map. Ask a partner a question about a place on the map.

Your partner points to the place and says, "Here it is." Then write three questions.

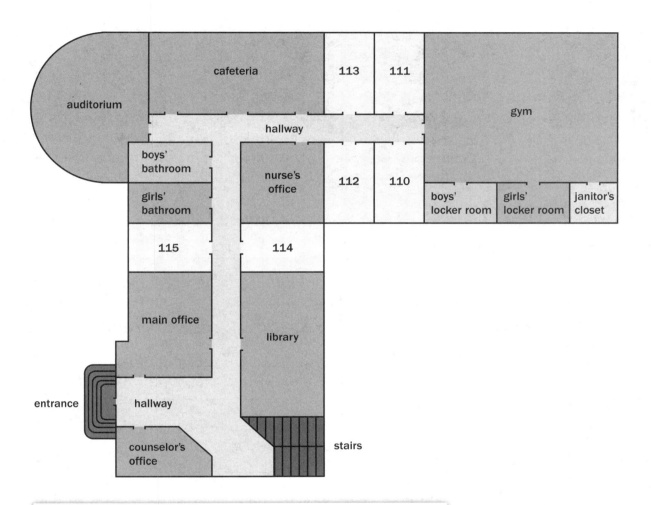

Questions

1. Where is the _____?

2. Where is Room _____?

3. Where's _____ _____?

4. _____ _____ the _____?

Name_____

Ask and Answer Questions

 Write words to finish each question. Then give your paper to a partner.

Answer your partner's questions.  Say each question and answer.

Mrs. Martinez
Principal

Mrs. Hasan
Counselor

Mr. Carrido
Secretary

Mr. Koval
Janitor

1. Who is the ___secretary___?

___Mr. Carrido___ is the ___secretary___.

2. Who _____ the counselor?

_____ is the

_____.

3. _____ is _____ _____?

_____ _____ the

_____.

4. Who is ___Mr. Koval___?

___Mr. Koval___ is the ___janitor___.

5. Who _____ Mrs. Martinez?

_____ is the

_____.

6. _____ is _____?

_____ _____ the

_____.

© NGSP & H

Name _____

High Frequency Words

A. Read each word aloud.  Then write it in the boxes.

1. c a n

2. p l a y   I ___can___ ___play___ softball in P.E.

3. t h a t   Do you like ___that___ sport?

B. Write the missing words.

4. _____ is the school nurse.

5. _____ we go to the library?

6. I _____ _____ the piano.

7. _____ is the _____.

8. The teacher _____ _____ the piano, too.

Write Words

A. Look at the words.

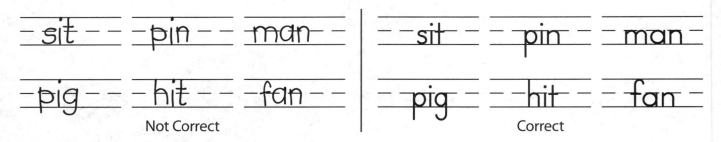

sit pin man	sit pin man
pig hit fan	pig hit fan
Not Correct	Correct

B. Trace each word. Then write it.

1. sit

2. pin

3. man

4. pig

5. hit

6. fan

7. it

8. an

© NGSP & H

Name _____

Write Words

A. 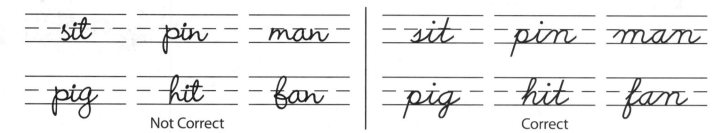 Look at the words.

sit	*pin*	*man*
pig	*hit*	*fan*
	Not Correct	

sit	*pin*	*man*
pig	*hit*	*fan*
	Correct	

B.  Trace each word. Then write it.

1. *sit*

2. *pin*

3. *man*

4. *pig*

5. *hit*

6. *fan*

7. *it*

8. *an*

Name _____

Reread and Retell

Write main ideas and details from *Time and Routines* on the lines below.

Under each main idea, write details about it.

We tell time with clocks and calendars.
Clocks use hours and minutes.

We do the same things at the same time.
Pablo gets up at 7 o'clock in the morning.

© NGSP & H

Write About Your First Day in the U.S.A.

A. Write about your first day in the United States. Draw pictures or tape photos in the boxes. Label your pictures. Tell where you are. Tell who you meet.

My First Day in the U.S.A.

by

I am in

The day is _____.
The time is _____.

I am at
I meet

The day is _____.
The time is _____.

B. Check the writing. Do you need to add a capital letter for the names of cities and streets? Do you need to add capital letters for the names of people and days of the week? Do you need to capitalize *I*?

Name _____

Give Information

Fill out the *I am* column. Work with a partner. Share your information with your partner. Then write your partner's information in the *You are* column.

	I am	You are
1. Tell your name.		
2. Tell where you are from.		
3. Tell what class you are in.		
4. Tell one more thing about yourself.		

© NGSP &

High Frequency Words

A. 🗨 Read each word aloud. ✍ Then write it.

1. can	_____	**4.** write	_____
2. play	_____	**5.** read	_____
3. that	_____	**6.** answer	_____

B. ✍ Write the letters.

7. Which words have 4 letters?

_p_ _l_ _a_ _y_

___ ___ ___ ___

___ ___ ___ ___

8. Which word has an **i**?

___ ___ ___ ___ ___

9. Which word has 3 letters?

___ ___ ___

10. Which word starts with **r**?

___ ___ ___ ___

11. Which word has an **l**?

___ ___ ___ ___

12. Which word starts with **a**?

___ ___ ___ ___ ___ ___

C. ✍ Write the missing word.

13. When do you _____play_____ soccer?
(can / play)

14. I _____ play it in P.E.
(can / write)

15. _____ sounds like fun.
(Answer / That)

16. I _____ in English.
(that / read)

17. I _____ in English, too.
(write / that)

18. I got the right _____.
(answer / play)

Name _____

Write Sentences

A. 👓 Look at the sentences.

Not Correct

What time is it?

Correct

What time is it?

B. ✏️ Trace each sentence. Then write it.

1. Is it time to play? _____

2. No, it is not. _____

3. It is time to read. _____

4. It is time to write. _____

5. It is not the time. _____

6. It is not the day. _____

7. When do we play? _____

8. Tomorrow we play. _____

© NGSP &

Name _____

Write Sentences

A. 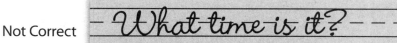 Look at the sentences.

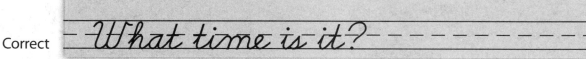

Not Correct — *What time is it?*

Correct — *What time is it?*

B. Trace each sentence. Then write it.

1. *Is it time to play?* — — — — — — —
2. *No, it is not.* — — — — — — —
3. *It is time to read.* — — — — — — —
4. *It is time to write.* — — — — — — —
5. *It is not the time.* — — — — — — —
6. *It is not the day.* — — — — — — —
7. *When do we play?* — — — — — — —
8. *Tomorrow we play.* — — — — — — —

Give Information

 Look at each picture.   Say the words that finish each sentence.
Then write the words.

1.

_____She_____ _____is_____ a bus driver.

2.

That is a ball. _____ _____ on the water.

3.

_____ _____ in the cafeteria.

4.

_____ _____ from South Korea.

5.

That is a computer. _____ _____ on

the steps.

6.

_____ _____ in the gym.

     © NGSP &

Name_____

Ask and Answer Questions

 Look at each picture. Say the words that finish each
question and answer. Then write the words.

1.

____Can____ John swim?

__Yes__, __he__ __can__.

3.

_____ Mike ride a skateboard?

_____, _____ _____.

2.

Can you __throw__ a ball?

__Yes__, __I__ _____.

4.

_____ the dog catch the ball?

_____, _____ _____.

High Frequency Words

A. Read each word aloud. 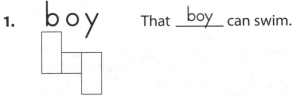 Then write it in the boxes.

1. b o y   That __boy__ can swim.

2. H e   __He__ swims well.

3. g i r l   Can that __girl__ swim, too?

B. 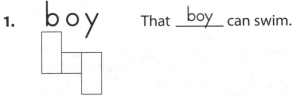 Write the missing words.

4. The _____ is in the gym.

5. The _____ is at the park.

6. _____ can sit in a _____.

7. Show me the _____ in the chair.

© NGSP &

Lil naps in class.

It is the last class.

Lil naps in class.

Illustrated by Ben Shannon © NGSP & HB

Lil's Last Class

Lil sits in Mr. Pit's class.

(title)

Words for People and Things

  Look at each picture. Say the word that finishes each sentence.

 Then write the word. Use *I*, *you*, *he*, *she*, *it*, *we*, or *they*.

1.

_____She_____ sings a song.

2.

_____ play music.

3.

_____ is a teacher.

4.

_____ am at school.

5.

Are _____ in my class?

6.

_____ is my ball.

7.

_____ play soccer.

8.

_____ can throw a ball.

Name _____

Give Information

 Look at each picture.   Say the words that finish each sentence.

 Then write the words. Use *he is, she is, it is,* or *they are.*

1. __They__ __are__ on the bench.

4. _____ _____ the coach.

2. _____ _____ a soccer player.

5. _____ _____ on the fiel

3. _____ _____ at the game.

6. Where is the ball? __ _____ on the field.

© NGSP &

Give Information

 Look at each picture. Say the words that finish each sentence.

 Then write the words.

1.

_____I_____ _____can_____ play the piano.

4.

_____ _____ play the drums.

2.

_____They_____ _____ sing.

5.

_____ _____ write a story.

3.

_____ _____ play the guitar.

6.

_____ _____ take a picture.

High Frequency Words

A. 🗨 Read each word aloud.   ✏ Then write it.

1. he	_____	**4.** they	_____
2. she	_____	**5.** boy	_____
3. we	_____	**6.** girl	_____

B. ✏ Write the letters.

7. Which words have 3 letters?

b   o   y

___   ___   ___

8. Which word has an **i**?

___   ___   ___   ___

9. Which words have 2 letters?

___   ___

___   ___

10. Which words have 4 letters?

___   ___   ___   ___

___   ___   ___   ___

C. ✏ Write the missing word.

11. Marta is a _____girl_____.
           (boy / girl)

12. _____ is a girl in my class.
    (She / He)

13. Raúl is a _____.
           (boy / girl)

14. _____ is a boy in my class.
    (She / He)

15. _____ play soccer.
    (We / Boy)

16. _____ run on a track.
    (They / He)

Tim and Lil

© NGSP & HB

Lil can play!

This is Tim at school.

© NGSP & HB

This is it!

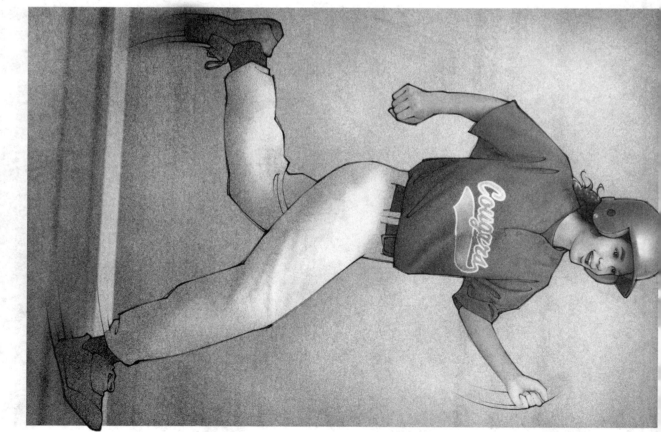

3

This is Lil. She sits at school.

© NGSP & HB

She hit it!

It is 3:00.

Tim has a mitt.

© NGSP & HB

Lil has a bat.

Name _____

Reread and Retell

Make a concept map to tell what kids like to do. In each oval, write a way that kids do things. For each way, write things kids do.

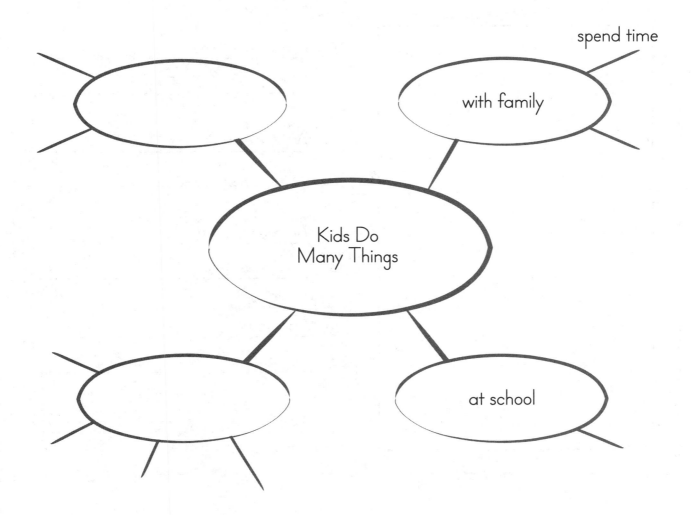

spend time

with family

Kids Do
Many Things

at school

Name _____

Write About a Classmate

A. ✏️ Write about a classmate. Draw a picture of a classmate you will talk to. Write four questions.

🤚 Ask a classmate your questions. ✏️ Then write the answers.

An Interview with _____

Q. What is _____

A. _____

Q. Where are _____

A. _____

Q. Where do _____

A. _____

Q. Can you _____

A. _____

B. 👓 Check the writing. Do you need to add a question mark to the end of each question?

Do you need to add a capital letter to the beginning of each sentence?

Do you need to add a period at the end of each answer?

© NGSP &

Give Information

 Look at each picture.    Say the words that finish each sentence.

 Then write the words.

1.

What is this? ____This____ ____is____ a bean.

2.

What are those? _____ ____are____

bananas.

3.

What are these? _____ _____

apples.

4.

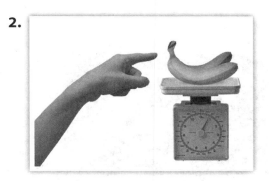

What is that? _____ _____

an orange.

5.

What are those? _____ _____

_____.

6.

What is this? _____ _____ _____

_____.

Name_____

High Frequency Words

A. 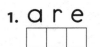 Read each word aloud. 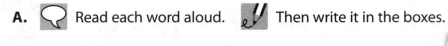 Then write it in the boxes.

1. a r e   We ____are____ at the store.

2. f o o d   We shop for ____food____.

3. s o m e   Would you like ____some____ apples?

B. 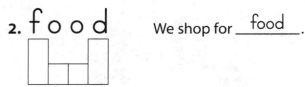 Write the missing words.

4. We _____ in the cafeteria.

5. This _____ is good.

6. Here _____ _____ oranges.

7. They _____ good _____.

© NGSP & H

Name _____

Letters and Sounds

A. Study the new letters and sounds.

Rr　　**Dd**　　**Cc**　　**Vv**　　**Oo**

B. 👂 Listen to each word. What letter spells the <u>first</u> sound you hear? ✏️ Circle the letter.

1.

   m　(d)　o

2.

   r　v　n

3.

   l　h　c

4.

   a　r　d

5.

   c　n　v

6.

   o　r　i

7.

   l　g　c

8.

   h　t　p

9.

   r　d　f

10.

    a　v　l

11.

    d　a　s

12.

    v　i　h

13.

    c　p　t

14.

    o　m　v

15.

    o　d　i

16.

    d　g　v

Letters and Sounds

 Say the name of each picture below.   Write the missing letters.

1.

<u>d</u> <u>o</u> <u>t</u>

2.

___ ___ ___ ___

3.

___ <u>o</u> ___

4.

___ ___ ___

5.

___ ___ ___

6.

<u>f</u> ___ <u>l</u> ___ ___

7.

<u>c</u> ___ <u>l</u> ___ <u>s</u> <u>s</u>

8.

___ <u>a</u> ___

9.

___ <u>a</u> ___

10.

___ ___ <u>m</u> <u>p</u>

11.

___ ___ ___

12.

___ ___ ___

© NGSP & H

Food

A.  Read each word.   Draw a line to match the word and the picture.

1.

apple

banana

beans

2.

bread

cheese

corn

3.

lettuce

milk

onion

B. Write the name.

4.

lettuce

6.

8.

5.

7.

9.

Express Likes and Dislikes

 Look at each picture. Do you like this food?   Write *I like* or *I don't like* to complete each sentence.

1.

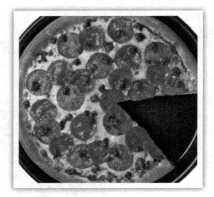

_____ I like _____ pizza.

2.

_____ carrots.

3.

_____ chicken.

4.

_____ cheese.

5.

_____ salad.

6.

_____ tacos.

 © NGSP & H

Name _____

High Frequency Words

A.  Read each word aloud.   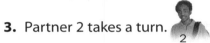 Then write it.

1. an _____ 4. a _____

2. of _____ 5. some _____

3. are _____ 6. food _____

B.   **How to Play**

1. Play with a partner. Each partner chooses a sign. X O

2. Partner 1 reads a word and marks the square with a sign.

3. Partner 2 takes a turn.

4. Get 3 Xs or Os in a row to win.

Game A

an	food	a
some	of	are
she	we	he

Game C

a	he	we
food	some	an
of	she	are

Game B

some	they	an
girl	are	boy
of	food	a

Game D

boy	are	of
food	an	girl
they	a	some

Name _____

Words with Short *a, i,* and *o*

A. 👓 Read each word.   ✍ Draw a line to match the word and the picture.

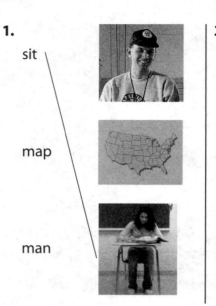

1.
sit

map

man

2.
pan

pig

pin

3.
dot

pot

mop

B. ✍ Write the missing words.

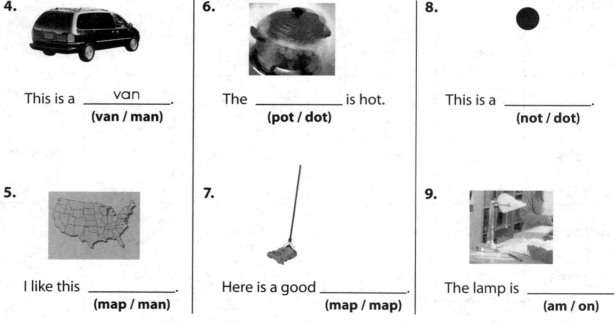

4.

This is a ___van___.
(van / man)

6.

The _____ is hot.
(pot / dot)

8.

This is a _____.
(not / dot)

5.

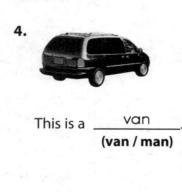

I like this _____.
(map / man)

7.

Here is a good _____.
(map / map)

9.

The lamp is _____.
(am / on)

   © NGSP & H

Words with Short *a, i,* and *o*

A. Write the missing letters. Then read the words in each list. How are they different?

1. <u>c</u> <u> </u> <u> </u>

 <u> </u> <u> </u> <u> </u>

 <u> </u> <u> </u> <u> </u>

2. <u>p</u> <u> </u> <u> </u>

 <u> </u> <u> </u> <u> </u>

 <u> </u> <u> </u> <u> </u> <u> </u>

3. <u>h</u> <u> </u> <u> </u>

 <u> </u> <u> </u> <u> </u>

 <u> </u> <u> </u> <u> </u>

B. Read each question. What word goes in the answer? Write the word. Then circle the correct picture.

4. Is this pot hot?

No, the <u>p</u> <u>o</u> <u>t</u> is not hot.

5. Is this your cap?

Yes, it is my ____ ____ ____.

6. Where is the mop?

The ____ ____ ____ is here.

7. Where can I sit?

You can ____ ____ ____ here.

8. Where is the dot?

The ____ ____ ____ is here!

9. Do you like the hat?

Yes, I like the ____ ____ ____.

Money

A. Read each word. Draw a line to match the word and the picture.

1.

one dollar

ten dollars

five dollars

2.

nickel

quarter

dime

B. Look at each picture. 💬 Say the word that finishes each sentence.
 Then write the word.

3.

These are ___bills___.

5.

These are _____.

7.

This is a _____.

4.

This is _____.

6.

This is a _____.

8.

This is a _____.

 © NGSP & H

Name _____

Buy and Sell

 Look at each picture. Say the words that finish each question and answer. Then write the words.

1.
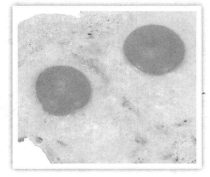

How much are these ___eggs__ ?

The eggs __are__ $4.75.

2.

How much do ___they___ cost?

The tacos _____ $1.20 each.

3.

How much do _____ cost?

The bagels _____ 95¢ each.

4.

How much is the _____?

The banana _____ 40¢.

5.

How much is the _____?

The salad _____ $5.00.

6.

How much do _____ cost? Two hot

dogs _____ $4.50.

High Frequency Words

A. 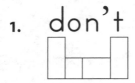 Read each word aloud.   Then write it in the boxes.

1. don't

2. like

I <u>don't</u> <u>like</u> hot dogs.

3. these

Do you like <u>these</u> foods?

B. Write the missing words.

4. Do you _____ those shoes?

5. I _____ like those shoes.

6. I _____ _____ shoes better.

7. Do you _____ _____ foods?

8. I _____ know. I will try them.

   © NGSP & H

Name _____

Write Words

A. 👓 Look at the words.

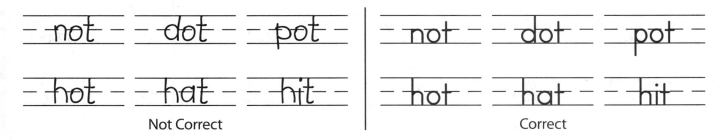

not   dot   pot | not   dot   pot
hot   hat   hit | hot   hat   hit

Not Correct | Correct

B. ✍ Trace each word. Then write it.

1. not

2. dot

3. pot

4. hot

5. hat

6. hit

7. on

8. in

Name_____

Write Words

A.  Look at the words.

not	dot	pot	not	dot	pot
hot	hat	hit	hot	hat	hit

Not Correct | Correct

B. Trace each word. Then write it.

1. *not*

2. *dot*

3. *pot*

4. *hot*

5. *hat*

6. *hit*

7. *on*

8. *in*

© NGSP & H

Name _____

Reread and Retell

Make a sequence chain to tell where food comes from.

Use each box to tell about one place.

farm

↓

↓

↓

My Favorite Food

A. ✍ Write about your favorite food and what you need to make it.

Draw a picture or tape a photo of it in the box. Label your picture.

Tell why the food is your favorite.

I like

To make

My favorite food is

B. ✏ Check the writing. Do you need to add -s to make a word plural?

© NGSP & H

Name _____

Express Needs and Wants

 Look at each picture.   Say the words that finish each sentence.

 Then write the words.

1.

I ___want___ a book about sports.

2.

___ ___need___ an encyclopedia.

3.

___ _____ some

magazines.

4.

___ _____ _____ envelopes.

5.

I need _____ _____.

6.

___ _____ ___

_____.

Name _____

High Frequency Words

A. 🗨 Read each word aloud. ✍ Then write it.

1. like _____ 4. and _____

2. these _____ 5. good _____

3. don't _____ 6. those _____

B. ✍ Write the letters.

   7. Which word has 3 letters?
   a   n   d
   ‾‾‾ ‾‾‾ ‾‾‾

   8. Which words have an **s**?
   ‾‾‾ ‾‾‾ ‾‾‾ ‾‾‾ ‾‾‾

   ‾‾‾ ‾‾‾ ‾‾‾ ‾‾‾ ‾‾‾

   9. Which word ends in **t**?
   ‾‾‾ ‾‾‾ ‾‾‾ ‾‾‾

   10. Which words have 4 letters?
   ‾‾‾ ‾‾‾ ‾‾‾ ‾‾‾

   ‾‾‾ ‾‾‾ ‾‾‾ ‾‾‾

   ‾‾‾ ‾‾‾ ‾‾‾ ‾‾‾

   11. Which word starts with **l**?
   ‾‾‾ ‾‾‾ ‾‾‾ ‾‾‾

   12. Which words end in **d**?
   ‾‾‾ ‾‾‾ ‾‾‾

   ‾‾‾ ‾‾‾ ‾‾‾ ‾‾‾

C. ✍ Write the missing word.

13. This soup is _____.
                 (good / these)

14. I _____ eat lunch
      (and / don't)
in the cafeteria.

15. _____ are my friends.
   (Good / Those)

16. Give _____ bananas to
         (like / these)
them.

17. Do you _____ pizza?
        (like / those)

18. I like pizza _____ tacos.
         (and / don't)

© NGSP & H

Name _____

Write Sentences

A. Look at the statements.

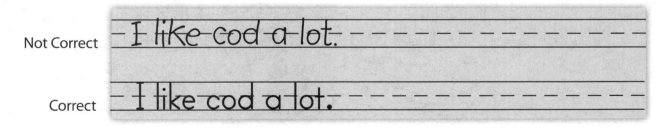

Not Correct — I like cod a lot. — — — — — — — —

Correct — I like cod a lot. — — — — — — — — —

B. Trace each sentence. Then write it.

1. I like cod and ham.

2. I like cod and figs.

3. I need cod and dip.

4. I like a lot of dip.

5. I want a tot to sip.

6. I like figs a lot.

7. What are these?

8. What are those?

Write Sentences

A. Look at the statements.

Not Correct   *I like cod a lot.*

Correct   *I like cod a lot.*

B. Trace each sentence. Then write it.

1. *I like cod and ham.* _____

2. *I like cod and figs.* _____

3. *I need cod and dip.* _____

4. *I like a lot of dip.* _____

5. *I want a lot to sip.* _____

6. *I like figs a lot.* _____

7. *What are these?* _____

8. *What are those?* _____

    © NGSP &

Give and Follow Commands

  Look at each picture. Say the words that finish each sentence.
Then write the words.

1.

___Call___ your friends.

2.

_____ three copies.

3.

_____ a picture.

4.

_____ to music.

5.

_____ a DVD.

6.

_____ _____ the monitor.

High Frequency Words

A. Read each word aloud.    Then write it in the boxes.

1. b o o k   This ___book___ is funny.

2. D o   ___Do___ you like to read?

3. D o e s   ___Does___ that book have pictures?

B.  Write the missing words.

4. They like this _____.

5. _____ Matt like it?

6. This is a good _____.

7. _____ you want it?

8. _____ she need a book?

     © NGSP &

Dot's cat, Pop, slips in.

Hop on the co Pop. Do not ho on top of me

We can both fit on the cot and nap.

Illustrated by Ben Shannon © NGSP & HB

(title)

Name _____

Give Commands

  Look at the signs.   Say the name of each sign.

Draw a picture of a sign in each box. Then write a command on each line.

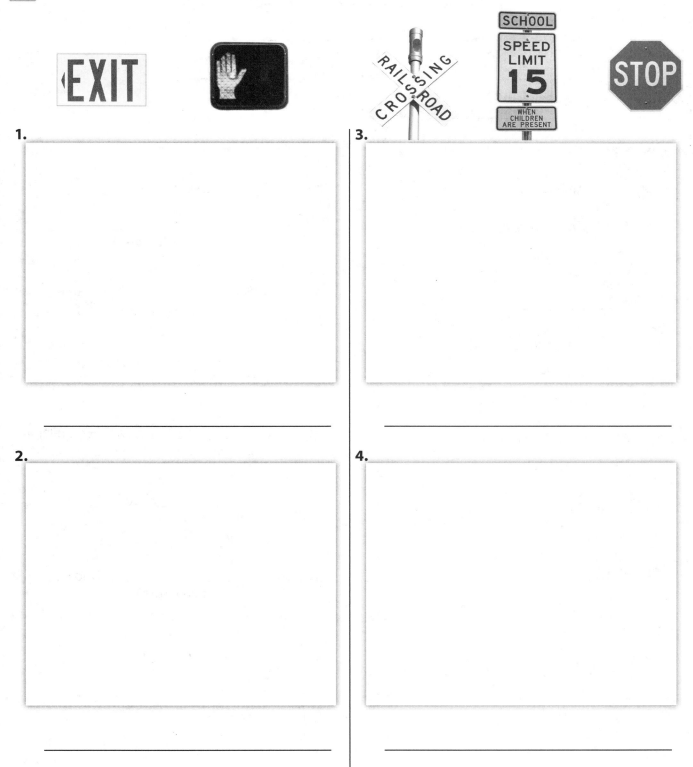

1.

_____

2.

_____

3.

_____

4.

_____

High Frequency Words

A. Read each word aloud. Then write it.

1. does	_____	**4.** picture	_____
2. how	_____	**5.** book	_____
3. both	_____	**6.** do	_____

B. Write the letters.

7. Which words have 4 letters?

d   o   e   s
___ ___ ___ ___
___ ___ ___ ___

8. Which words start with **d**?

___ ___

___ ___ ___ ___

9. Which word ends with **w**?

___ ___ ___

10. Which word has an **i**?

___ ___ ___ ___ ___ ___ ___

11. Which words start with **b**?

___ ___ ___ ___

___ ___ ___ ___

12. Which word has two **o**'s?

___ ___ ___ ___

C. Write the missing word.

13. Look at this _____.
   (do / book)

14. I like the _____ on it.
   (both / picture)

15. _____ much is it?
   (How / Does)

16. _____ it cost five dollars?
   (Does / Do)

17. _____ you want this
   (Does / Do)
book, too?

18. I want _____ books.
   (how / both)

© NGSP &

Dot and Ron

© NGSP & HB

Dot hops on the beam.

© NGSP & HB

Ron hops off.
He is on the mat.

Ron hops on the rings.

© NGSP & HB

3

Dot hops off.
She is on the mat.

Look at Dot!

© NGSP & HB

Look at Ron!

Name _____

Reread and Retell

Make a sequence chain to tell who learns the good news and how they get it.

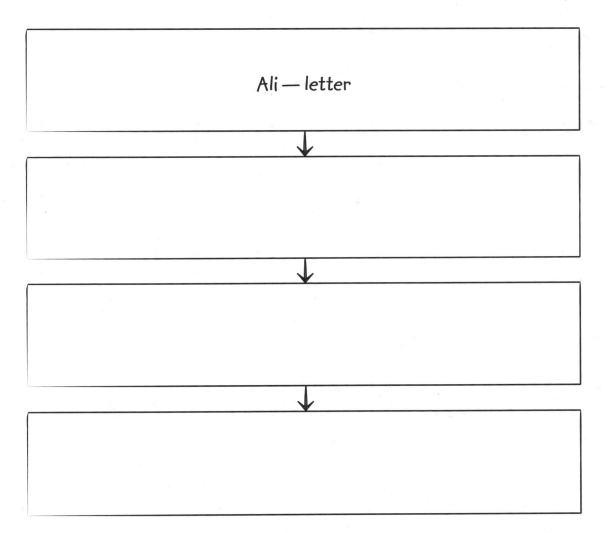

```
┌─────────────────────────────────────────────┐
│                                               │
│               Ali — letter                    │
│                                               │
└─────────────────────────────────────────────┘
                      │
                      ▼
┌─────────────────────────────────────────────┐
│                                               │
│                                               │
│                                               │
└─────────────────────────────────────────────┘
                      │
                      ▼
┌─────────────────────────────────────────────┐
│                                               │
│                                               │
│                                               │
└─────────────────────────────────────────────┘
                      │
                      ▼
┌─────────────────────────────────────────────┐
│                                               │
│                                               │
│                                               │
└─────────────────────────────────────────────┘
```

How to Do Something

A. ✐ Write the steps for how to do something. Draw a picture in the box. Label your picture.

How to _____

1.

2.

3.

4.

5.

6.

B. 👓 Check the writing. Do you need to add any capital letters? Do you need to add a period or an exclamation point?

© NGSP & H

Parts of the Body

 Look at the picture. Say the word for each part of the body.
Then write the word.

1. head

2. _____

3. _____

4. _____

5. _____

6. _____

7. _____

8. _____

9. _____

10. _____

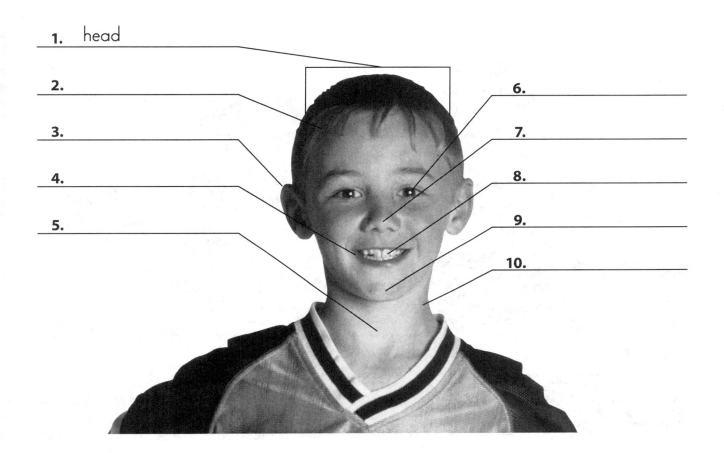

Describe Yourself

A.  Look at the picture. Say the words that finish each sentence.

Then write the words.

1. I ___am___ ___tall___.

2. I am _____.

3. I _____ _____ _____.

4. My _____ _____ _____.

5. My _____ _____ _____.

B. Draw a picture of a yourself. Then write two sentences that tell what you look like.

I am _____.

My _____ _____ _____.

© NGSP & H

Describe Other People

 Look at each picture. Say the words that finish each sentence.

 Then write the words.

1.

__He__ __is__ tall.

2.

_____ _____ young.

3.

_____ has long hair.

4.

_____ _____ _____ hair.

5.

_____ eyes _____ brown.

6.

_____ _____ _____ blond.

Name_____

High Frequency Words

A. Read each word aloud.   Then write it in the boxes.

1. g e t   She wants to ___get___ new glasses.

2. h a s   She __has__ brown hair.

3. o l d   These glasses are __old__.

B. Write the missing words.

4. He wants to _____ lunch.

5. She _____ a sandwich.

6. The _____ ball _____ a hole.

7. He needs to _____ a new ball.

8. He can't kick the _____ ball.

© NGSP & H

Letters and Sounds

A. Study the new letters and sounds.

Jj

Bb

Ww

Kk

Ee

B. **How to Play**

1. Write the letters from the box. Write one letter in each square.

2. Then listen to the word your teacher reads.

3. Put a ◯ on the letter that stands for the first sound in the word.

4. The first player to cover all the letters in a row is the winner.

Letters to Write

a	i	p
b	j	r
b	j	s
c	k	t
d	k	v
e	l	w
f	m	w
g	n	
h	o	

Words to Read

am	got	lot	top
bat	hit	mat	van
big	it	not	win
can	jam	on	wig
dot	jog	pin	
egg	kid	red	
fat	kit	sit	

Name_____

Letters and Sounds

 Say the name of each picture below. What letter spells the <u>first</u> sound you hear? Write the letter.

1.

____p____

2.

_____

3.

_____

4.
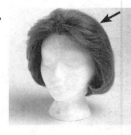
_____

5.

_____

6.

_____

7.

_____

8.

_____

9.

_____

10.
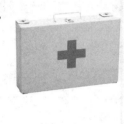
_____

11.

_____

12.

_____

© NGSP & H

Name _____

Express Feelings

 Look at each picture. 💬 Say the words that finish each question and answer. 🖊 Then write the words.

1. How do you feel?

I feel _____fine_____.

3. How _____ _____ _____?

I _____ _____.

I have a _____.

2. How do _____ _____?

I feel _____.

My _____ hurts.

4. _____ _____ _____ feel?

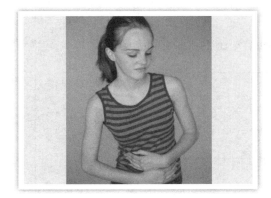

I feel _____. ____ _____

____ stomachache.

High Frequency Words

A. 🗨 Read each word aloud.   ✍ Then write it.

1. have	_____	**4.** old	_____
2. call	_____	**5.** great	_____
3. has	_____	**6.** get	_____

B. ✍ Write the letters.

7. Which words have 3 letters?

o l d
____ ____ ____

____ ____ ____

____ ____ ____

8. Which words have an **e**?

____ ____ ____

____ ____ ____ ____

____ ____ ____ ____ ____

9. Which words have 4 letters?

____ ____ ____ ____

____ ____ ____ ____

10. Which word has 5 letters?

____ ____ ____ ____ ____

11. Which word ends with **d**?

____ ____ ____

C. ✍ Write the missing word.

12. She _____ brown hair.
(has / old)

13. I _____ long hair.
(have / has)

14. My hairstyle is _____.
(get / old)

15. I will _____ my mother.
(call / great)

16. I will _____ a hair cut.
(get / old)

17. It will look _____.
(has / great)

   © NGSP & H

Name_____

Words with Short *a, i, o,* and *e*

A. Read each word. Draw a line to match the word and the picture.

1.

jam

ham

hat

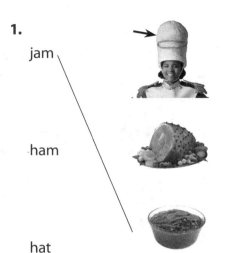

2.

pen

ten

men

3.

cat

bat

bed

B.  Write the missing word.

4.

Here are two _____.
        (men / ten)

5.

• • • • •
• • • • •

There are

_____ dots.
(ten / pen)

6.

My pet is a _____.
            (pig / pin)

7.

This is a good _____.
              (pan / pen)

8.

He can _____
       (hot / hit)

the 🔴.

9.

This is my _____.
           (cap / map)

10.

Here is a _____.
          (bed / Ed)

11.

I do _____
     (dot / not)

like to play.

12.

Put it in the _____.
              (pot / pat)

Name _____

Words with Short *a, i, o,* and *e*

A. Write the missing letters. 💬 Then read the words in each list. How are the words different?

1. m _____ _____ _____

 _____ _____ _____

 _____ _____ _____

2. c _____ _____

 _____ _____ _____

 _____ _____ _____

3. p _____ _____

 _____ _____ _____

 _____ _____ _____

B. Write the missing letters.

4.

This is my __p__ __e__ __n__ .

5.

Look at the

_____ _____ _____ .

6.

Here is my _____ _____ _____ .

7.

Carlos has a _____ _____ _____ .

8.

Do you like my

_____ _____ __s__ __t__ ?

9.

This is a

__f__ __l__ _____ _____ .

10.

I like to _____ _____ _____ .

11.

I _____ _____ _____ at my

_____ _____ _____ _____ .

12.

Where is my

_____ _____ _____ ?

 © NGSP & H

Name _____

Express Feelings

 Look at each picture.  Say the words that finish each question
and answer.  Then write the words.

1. How do you feel?

I feel __proud__.

4. How _____ _____ feel?

I feel _____.

2. How do you _____?

I feel

_____.

5. How _____ _____ _____?

I _____

_____.

3. How do _____ _____?

_____ am

_____.

6. _____ _____ _____ _____?

_____ _____

_____.

Name _____

High Frequency Words

A. Read each word aloud. Then write it in the boxes.

1. feel

2. very   We ___feel___ __very__ happy!

3. too   Do you want to play, __too__?

B. Write the missing words.

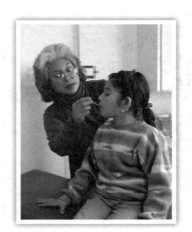

4. How do you _____?

5. I feel _____ good.

6. I _____ very good, _____.

7. We _____ _____ proud!

8. Our coach feels _____ proud, _____.

     © NGSP & H

Write Words

A. 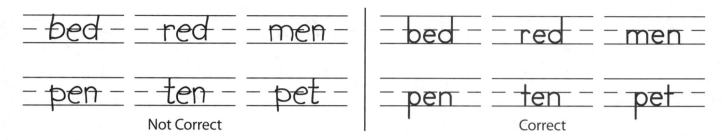 Look at the words.

bed — red — men	bed — red — men
pen — ten — pet	pen — ten — pet
Not Correct	Correct

B. Trace each word. Then write it.

1. bed

2. red

3. men

4. pen

5. ten

6. pet

7. pat

8. pot

Name _____

Write Words

A. Look at the words.

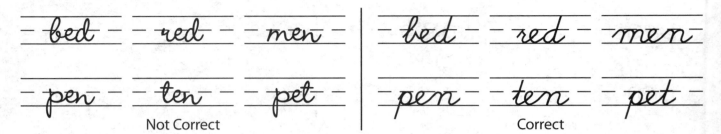

Not Correct   Correct

B. Trace each word. Then write it.

1. bed

2. red

3. men

4. pen

5. ten

6. pet

7. pat

8. pot

© NGSP &

Name _____

Reread and Retell

Make a concept map to tell how people keep fit. In each oval, write one thing that keeps people fit. For each thing, write examples.

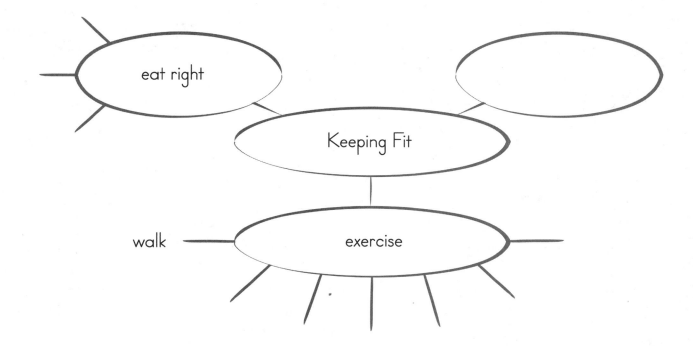

Name _____

Describe a Friend

A. Write about a friend. Tell what your friend looks like.

Draw pictures or tape photos in the boxes.

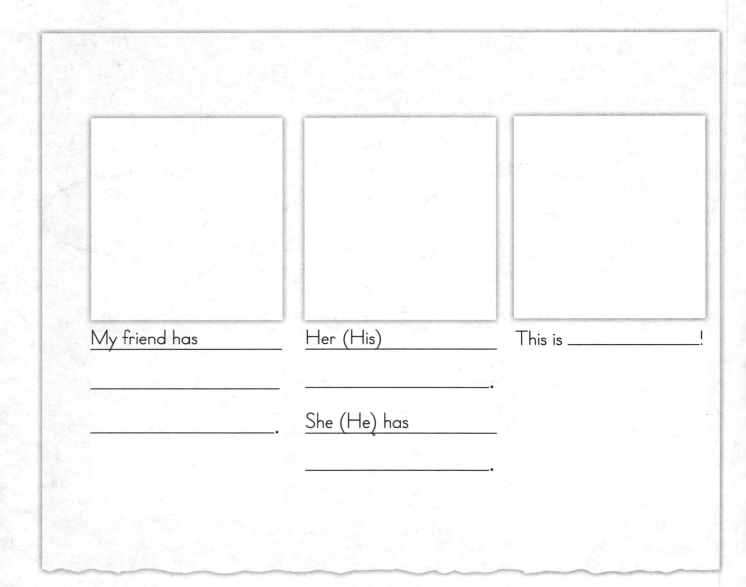

My friend has _____

_____

_____.

Her (His) _____

_____.

She (He) has _____

_____.

This is _____!

B. Check the writing. Do you need to use *he* or *his* to describe a man or a boy?

Do you need to use *she* or *her* to describe a woman or a girl?

© NGSP &

Ask and Answer Questions

 Look at each picture. Say the words that finish each question and answer. Then write the words.

1.

<u>Does</u> the <u>shirt</u> <u>have</u> a collar?
<u>Yes, it does</u>.

2.

_____ the _____ _____ a pocket?
_____.

3.

_____ the _____ _____ buttons?
_____.

4.

<u>Do</u> the <u>skirts</u> <u>have</u> pockets?
<u>No, they do not</u>.

5.

_____ the _____ _____ pockets?
_____.

6.

_____ the _____ _____ collars?
_____.

High Frequency Words

A. 🗨 Read each word aloud. ✍ Then write it.

1. feel	_____	**4.** too	_____
2. put	_____	**5.** things	_____
3. very	_____	**6.** your	_____

B. ✍ Write the letters.

7. Which words have an **r**?

y o u r
___ ___ ___ ___

___ ___ ___ ___

8. Which words have 3 letters?

___ ___ ___

___ ___ ___

9. Which words have 4 letters?

___ ___ ___ ___

___ ___ ___ ___

___ ___ ___ ___

10. Which word has 6 letters?

___ ___ ___ ___ ___ ___

C. ✍ Write the missing word.

11. How do you _____?
        (feel / too)

12. I am _____ sick.
        (things / very)

13. I feel bad, _____.
        (too / your)

14. Take your _____ home.
        (very / things)

15. I _____ them on the table.
        (put / feel)

16. Don't forget _____ bag.
        (your / put)

  © NGSP &

Write Sentences

A. Look at the sentences.

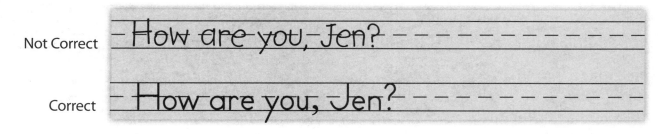

Not Correct   How are you, Jen?

Correct   How are you, Jen?

B. Trace each sentence. Then write it.

1. How are you, Kit?

2. We feel great!

3. We feel fit.

4. We hop on the mat.

5. We tag and we kid.

6. We do the jig.

7. We jab at the bag.

8. We feel very fit!

Name _____

Write Sentences

A. 👀 Look at the sentences.

Not Correct — How are you, Jen?

Correct — How are you, Jen?

B. ✍ Trace each sentence. Then write it.

1. How are you, Kit? _____

2. We feel great! _____

3. We feel fit! _____

4. We hop on the mat. _____

5. We tag and we kid. _____

6. We do the jig. _____

7. We jab at the bag. _____

8. We feel very fit! _____

© NGSP &

Name _____

Clothing and Colors

How to Play

1. Color each piece of clothing.

2. Play with a partner.   Each partner chooses a sign. X O

3. Partner 1 says the color and name of a piece of clothing and marks the square with his or her sign.

4. Then Partner 2 takes a turn.

5. Get 3 Xs or Os in a row to win.

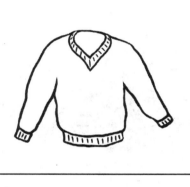  

  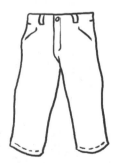

Describe Things

 Look at each picture. Say the words that finish each sentence.
Then write the words.

1.

Here is a __belt__.

It has ___a___ __big__ __buckle__.

2.

Here is ___a___ __T-shirt__.

It _____ _____ sleeves.

3.

Here _____ _____ _____.

It _____ _____.

4.

Here are some _____.

They have _____ _____.

5.

Here are _____ _____.

They _____ _____.

6.

Here _____ _____ _____.

_____ _____ _____.

© NGSP &

Name _____

Ask and Answer Questions

 Look at each picture. Say the words that complete each question and answer. Then write the words.

1.

Which _____shirt_____ do you like?

I like _____this_____ shirt.

3.

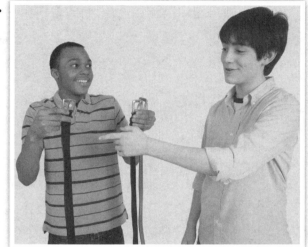

_____ _____ do you like?

_____ _____ _____ belt.

2.

Which _____ do you like?

I like _____ pants.

4.

_____ jeans _____ _____

_____? _____ _____

_____ jeans.

High Frequency Words

A. Read each word aloud. Then write it in the boxes.

1. h e l p   I need your ___help___.

2. g r o u p   Will your ___group___ of friends come?

3. w o r k   Please ___work___ with us.

B. Write the missing words.

4. We _____ each other.

5. Our _____ works hard.

6. Do you want to _____ with our _____?

7. We need _____.

8. We help with this _____.

Ben gets in.

Ted gets in!

Illustrated by Ben Shannon © NGSP & HB

Ben and Ted sit in the sand.

(title)

Name _____

Express Ideas

 Look at each picture.   Say the words that finish each sentence.

Then write the words.

1.

It's ____snowy____ today.

I need to wear ___boots___.

2.

It's ____hot____ today.

I want to wear _____.

3.

_____ _____ today.

I _____ _____ wear a _____.

4.

_____ _____ today.

I _____ _____ wear a _____.

5.

_____ _____ _____.

I _____ _____ wear a _____.

6.

_____ _____ _____.

I _____ _____ wear a _____.

High Frequency Words

A. 💬 Read each word aloud.   ✍ Then write it.

---

1. little _____   **4.** them _____

2. help _____   **5.** with _____

3. group _____   **6.** need _____

B. ✍ Write the letters.

7. Which words have 4 letters?

 t   h   e   m
___ ___ ___ ___

___ ___ ___ ___

___ ___ ___ ___

___ ___ ___ ___

8. Which word has a **w**?

___ ___ ___ ___

9. Which words have an **e**?

___ ___ ___ ___

___ ___ ___ ___

___ ___ ___ ___

___ ___ ___ ___ ___

10. Which words have a **p**?

___ ___ ___ ___

___ ___ ___ ___

C. ✍ Write the missing word.

11. I _____ to get directions.
(little / need)

12. I will give _____ to you.
(with / them)

13. Thanks, these will _____.
(help / with)

14. My house has a _____
(with / little)
garden.

15. I will bring my friends _____ me.
(with / them)

16. It will be a fun _____.
(group / need)

Where Is My Pen?

© NGSP & HB

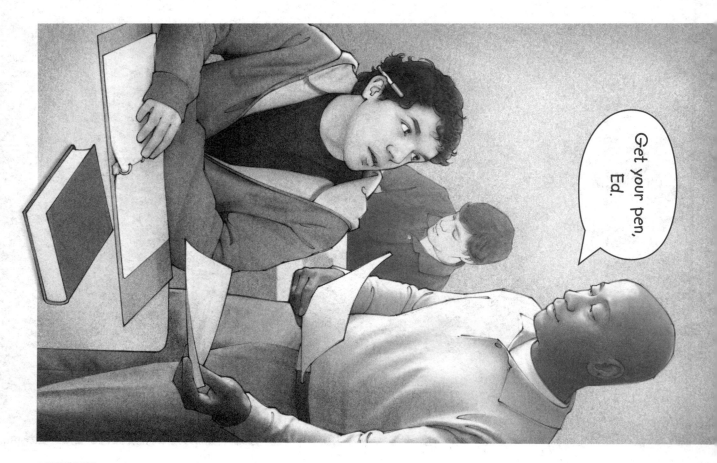

© NGSP & HB

3

© NGSP & HB

© NGSP & HB

Name_____

Reread and Retell

Make a concept map to tell about the shoes people wear. In the ovals, tell where and when people wear shoes. Then name the different kinds of shoes people might wear for that activity.

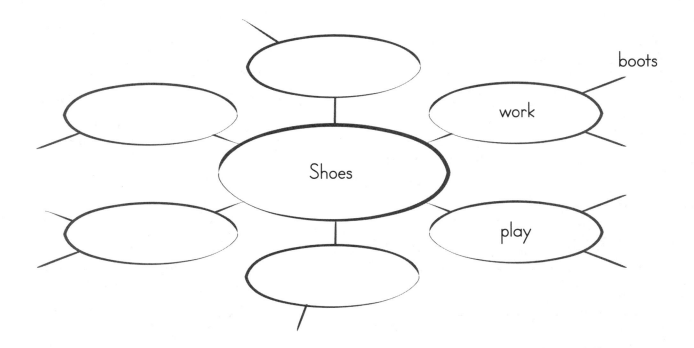

boots

work

Shoes

play

Write a Letter and a List

A. ✍ Your friend is coming to visit you. Write a letter to your friend. Tell your friend about the weather. Tell what clothes your friend needs to bring for the weather.

_____

Dear _____,

   I'm glad you are coming to _____ soon.
It's _____ _____.

Here is what you need to bring:

_____

_____

_____

_____

_____

                                        Your friend,

                              _____

B. ✏ Check the writing. Do you need to add a period or an exclamation point at the end of a sentence?

© NGSP & H

Name _____

Give Directions

Look at the map. You are at the supermarket. Say the words that finish each sentence in the directions. Then write the words.

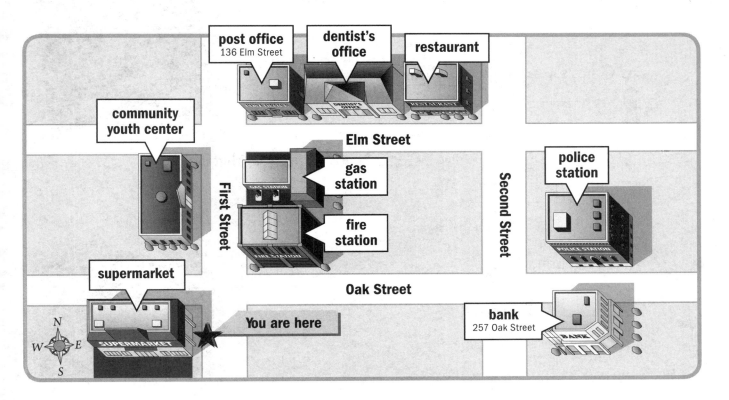

1. Where is the ___restaurant___?

Go up ___First Street___.

Go _____ block.

Turn _____ at

_____.

The restaurant is _____

_____ the dentist's office.

2. _____ _____

_____ bank?

Go one block on _____.

The bank is at _____.

It is _____ _____ the

police station.

Name_____

High Frequency Words

A. 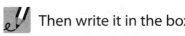 Read each word aloud. Then write it in the boxes.

1.   o n
     ☐☐

   I live ___on___ Third Street.

2.   W h e r e
     ☐☐☐☐☐

   _____Where_____ do you live?

3.   a r o u n d
     ☐☐☐☐☐☐

   I live ___around___ the corner from Third Street.

B. Write the missing words.

4.   _____ is the park?

5.   The park is _____ the corner.

6.   It is _____ Second Street.

7.   _____ is your house?

8.   I live _____ the corner, _____ First Street.

© NGSP & H

Letters and Sounds

A. Study the new letters and sounds.

| **Zz** | **Yy** | **Uu** | **Qu qu** | **Xx** |

B. **How to Play Bingo**

1. ✍️ Write the letters from the box. Write one letter in each square.

2. 👂 Then listen to the word your teacher reads.

3. ✍️ Put a ◯ on the letter that stands for the first sound in the word.

4. The first player to cover all the letters in a row is the winner.

Letters to Write

a	j	s
b	k	t
c	l	u
d	m	v
e	n	w
f	o	y
g	p	z
h	qu	
i	r	

Words to Read

am	him	on	van
bat	in	pen	wig
cot	jam	quit	yes
dot	kid	red	zip
egg	lot	sat	
fan	map	ten	
got	not	up	

Name_____

Letters and Sounds

 Say the name of each picture below. What letters spell the sounds you hear? Write the missing letters.

1.

_l_ _e_ _g_

5.

_c_ ___ ___

9.

___ ___

2.

___ ___ _i_ _l_ _t_

6.

___ ___ _l_

10.

___ ___ ___

3.

_a_ ___

7.

_r_ ___ _g_

11.

___ ___ ___

4.

_s_ ___ ___

8.

___ _u_ _s_

12.

___ ___ ___

© NGSP & H

Name _____

Express Intentions

 Look at each picture. Say the words that finish each sentence.

Then write the words.

1.

I __am__ __going__ __to__ buy

some apples. I __will__ make an apple

pie tomorrow.

2.

I __am__ _____ _____ buy some

shoes. I _____ wear them tonight.

3.

I _____ _____ _____ buy some

books. _____ _____ read them this

summer.

4.

_____ _____ _____ _____ buy

some flowers. _____ _____ give them to

my mom for her birthday.

High Frequency Words

A. 🗨 Read each word aloud. ✍ Then write it.

1. give _____	**4.** work _____
2. take _____	**5.** around _____
3. on _____	**6.** where _____

B. ✍ Write the letters.

7. Which words end with an **e**?

w h e r e
___ ___ ___ ___ ___

___ ___ ___ ___

___ ___ ___ ___

8. Which words have a **w**?

___ ___ ___ ___ ___

___ ___ ___ ___

9. Which word has 6 letters?

___ ___ ___ ___ ___ ___

10. Which word has 2 letters?

___ ___

C. ✍ Write the missing word.

11. _____ is the library?
   (Around / Where)

12. The library is _____
   (take / on)
   the right.

13. I will _____ this book.
   (take / work)

14. I will look _____ for an
   (give / around)
   empty table.

15. I can _____ you my book.
   (give / where)

16. Thanks, that will help with my

   _____.
   (around / work)

© NGSP & H

Name _____

Words with Short *a, i, o, e,* and *u*

A. Read each word. Draw a line to match the word and the picture.

1.

cot

cat

cap

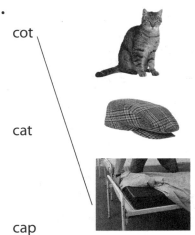

2.

up

cup

cut

3.

ax

ox

box

B. Write the missing word.

4.

I can __z__ __i__ __p__ it.

6.

I like this old

____ ____ ____ ____ ____.

8.

I have ____ ____ ____ pins.

5.

This is my ____ ____ ____.

7.

Do you like my little

____ ____ ____?

9.

Is this a pig?

____ ____ ____!

Name _____

Words with Short *a, i, o, e,* and *u*

A. Write the missing letters. 💬 Then read the words in each list. How are the words different?

1.

__ u __ p

→

___ ___ ___

___ ___ ___

2.

__ c __ ___ ___

___ ___ ___

___ ___ ___

3.

__ p __ ___

___ ___ ___

___ ___ ___

B. What word completes each sentence and tells about the picture? Spell the word.

4.

There is __ m _ i _ l _ k _

in my ___ ___ ___.

5.

Is this my ___ ___ ___?

6.

He ___ ___ ___ it.

7.

I have a

___ ___ ___ ___.

8.

She can ___ ___ ___ it.

9.

He has an ___ ___ ___.

10.

There is a bug on my

___ ___ ___.

11.

Here is an ___ ___.

12.

The lamp is not in the

___ ___ ___.

© NGSP & H

Describe Actions

A. Look at each picture. 🗨 Say the words that finish the sentence.
Then write the words.

1.

They ride ___bicycles___.

2.

They ride ___on___ _____

_____.

3.

They take _____ _____.

4.

They _____ _____ _____ car.

5.

They _____ _____.

6.

They _____ a _____.

Name _____

High Frequency Words

A. Read each word aloud. 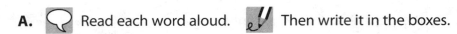 Then write it in the boxes.

1. to   We are going ___to___ study for the test.

2. Which   ___Which___ subject will we study?

3. here   Look ___here___, in your notebook.

B.  Write the missing words.

4. _____ is the ball.

5. We are going _____ play a game.

6. _____ team are you on?

7. _____ book are you going _____ read?

8. I am going _____ sit _____ and read this book.

   © NGSP & H

Name _____

Write Words

A. 👓 Look at the words.

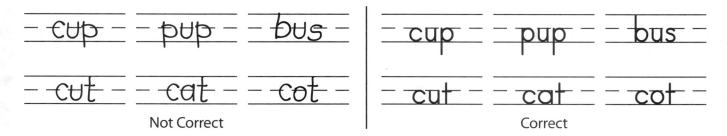

| cup | pup | bus | | cup | pup | bus |
| cut | cat | cot | | cut | cat | cot |

Not Correct   Correct

B. ✍ Trace each word. Then write it.

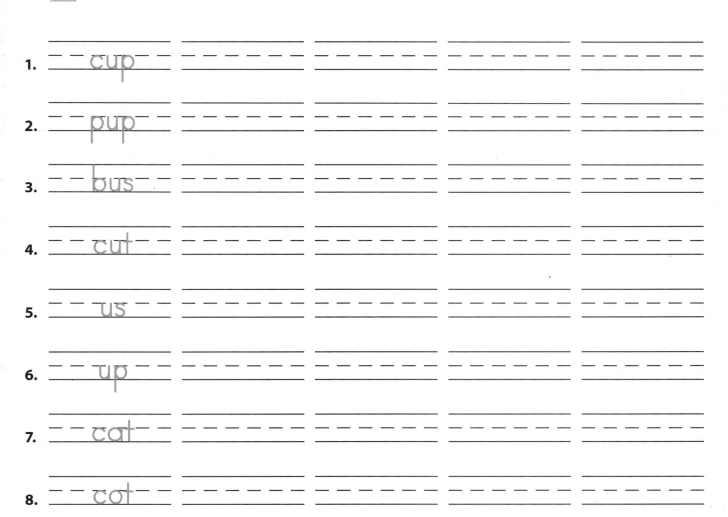

1. cup

2. pup

3. bus

4. cut

5. us

6. up

7. cat

8. cot

Name _____

Write Words

A. 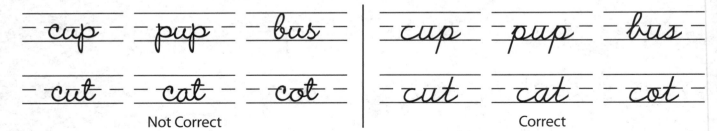 Look at the words.

cap pup bus	cap pup bus
cut cat cot	cut cat cot
Not Correct	Correct

B. Trace each word. Then write it.

1. _ap

2. pup

3. bus

4. cut

5. us

6. up

7. cat

8. cot

© NGSP & H

Reread and Retell

 Make a chart to show which vehicles have wheels and which do not.

Wheels	No Wheels
rickshaw	ferry

Write About Your Favorite Place

A. ✍ Write about your favorite place. Draw pictures or tape photos

of people and activities there. Label your pictures.

_____

I like _____. It is my favorite place.

(name of your favorite place)

I see _____   I _____   I _____

_____   _____   _____

_____.   _____.   _____.

B. 👓 Check the writing. Do you need to add nouns and describing words?

Do you need to put your words in the right order?

© NGSP & H

Name _____

Describe Actions

A. Look at each picture. 💬 Say the words that finish each sentence.
Then write the words.

1.

In the winter, he ___shovels___ snow. (shovel)

2.

In January, So Ying _____. (skate)

3.

In the spring, Tara _____ flowers. (plant)

4.

In October, she _____ leaves. (rake)

5.

In the summer, she _____ basketball. (play)

6.

In July, he _____ in the pool. (swim)

High Frequency Words

A. 🗨 Read each word aloud.   ✍ Then write it.

---

1. in   _____   4. here   _____

2. to   _____   5. will   _____

3. letters _____   6. which   _____

B. ✍ Write the letters.

7. Which words have an **e**?

l e t t e r s
h e r e

8. Which words have an **i**?

___ ___

___ ___ ___ ___

___ ___ ___ ___ ___

9. Which words have a **t**?

___ ___

___ ___ ___ ___ ___ ___ ___

10. Which words have 2 letters?

___ ___

___ ___

C. ✍ Write the missing word.

11. I am going _____to_____ the
　　　　　　(to / here)
shoe store.

12. I _____ buy a pair
　　　(will / which)
of shoes.

13. _____ shoes will
　　　(In / Which)
you buy?

14. They have _____
　　　　　　(will / letters)
on the side.

15. Can you get them _____?
　　　　　　　(here / which)

16. Let's go _____
　　　　　(in / letters)
the store and see.

   © NGSP & H

Name _____

Write Sentences

A. Look at the sentences.

Not Correct — What do you do on a hot day?

Correct — What do you do on a hot day?

B. Trace each sentence. Then write it.

1. We run around. _____

2. We sit in the sun. _____

3. We dig up yams. _____

4. We have some fun. _____

5. We read a book. _____

6. We get on a bus. _____

7. We work on the pup. _____

8. He got in the mud! _____

Write Sentences

A. Look at the sentences.

Not Correct *What do you do on a hot day?*

Correct *What do you do on a hot day?*

B. Trace each sentence. Then write it.

1. *We run around.* _____

2. *We sit in the sun.* _____

3. *We dig up yams.* _____

4. *We have some fun.* _____

5. *We read a book.* _____

6. *We get on a bus.* _____

7. *We work on the pup.* _____

8. *He got in the mud!* _____

© NGSP &

Describe Actions

  Look at each picture. Say the words that finish each sentence.
Then write the words.

1.

On New Year's Day, _____she_____
_____dances_____. (dance)

2.

On Valentine's Day, _____
_____ cards. (give)

3.

On New Year's Day, _____
_____ special clothes. (wear)

4.

On Thanksgiving Day, _____they_____
_____ a big meal. (eat)

5.

On Independence Day, _____
_____ the fireworks. (enjoy)

6.

On Day of the Dead, _____
_____ special bread. (bake)

Name _____

High Frequency Words

A. 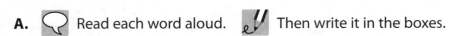 Read each word aloud.   Then write it in the boxes.

1. n i g h t
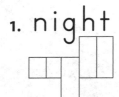

The ___night___ comes early in the winter.

2. t h i n k

I ___think___ I like spring best.

3. l a t e r

It gets dark ___later___ in spring.

4. f o r

Spring is best ___for___ planting a garden.

B. 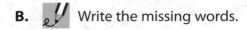 Write the missing words.

5. I _____ we will plant our garden tomorrow.

6. Spring weather is perfect _____ baseball, too.

7. We can play baseball _____ this evening.

8. At _____ we will sleep well.

© NGSP & I

_____
(title)

Make a Request

 Look at each picture.   Write the words that finish each question.

1.

_____Will_____ _____you_____ _____please_____
_____dance_____ with me?

2.

_____ _____
_____ _____make_____ a cake?

3.

_____ _____I_____ _____
the gift now?

4.

_____ _____
_____ _____share_____ this meal?

5.

_____ _____we_____ _____
for the party?

6.

_____ _____
_____ _____ this card?

High Frequency Words

A. 🗨 Read each word aloud. ✍ Then write it.

1. see	_____	**5.** night	_____
2. later	_____	**6.** think	_____
3. soon	_____	**7.** year	_____
4. for	_____		

B. ✍ Write the letters.

8. Which words have 5 letters?

t h i n k
— — — — —

— — — — —

— — — — —

9. Which words have an **i**?

— — — — —

— — — — —

10. Which words have an **o**?

— — —

— — — —

11. Which words have an **e**?

— — —

— — — —

— — — — —

C. ✍ Write the missing word.

12. I will visit my friends this

_____.
(year / for)

13. I hope to see them _____.
(soon / night)

14. I _____ they are a lot
(later / think)
of fun.

15. At _____, they ride a
(soon / night)
bus to the movies.

16. I like to _____ them.
(year / see)

17. I haven't seen them _____
(see / for)
two months.

18. I have to go, but I will call you

_____.
(later / think)

  © NGSP &

Where Is the Sun?

© NGSP & HB

At last, Jan has fun in the sun.

There is no sun. This is no fun for Jan.

© NGSP & HB

Here it is!

Jan will look for the sun.

© NGSP & HB

Jan looks up a book.

Jan gets on the bus.

© NGSP & HB

Jan runs up the steps.

Reread and Retell

Make two main idea diagrams. In the first, name each season and tell what its weather is like. In the second, write a type of weather and tell an activity people do in that weather.

Season	Weather
spring	rainy, windy

Weather	Activity
windy	fly a kite

Write About a Celebration

A. ✍ Write about your favorite celebration. Tell what makes this celebration special.

Draw pictures or tape photos in the boxes. Label your pictures.

_____

(Name of the Celebration)

by _____

In _____ we celebrate

_____. For _____,

we do special things.

My _____   We _____

B. ✂ Check the writing. Do you need to add -s at the end of verbs for *he, she,* or *it?*

© NGSP & H

S	S	S	S	S
M	M	M	M	M
F	F	F	F	F
H	H	H	H	H
T	T	T	T	T
A	A	A	A	A

NGSP & HB

s	s	s	s	s
m	m	m	m	m
f	f	f	f	f
h	h	h	h	h
t	t	t	t	t
a	a	a	a	a

© NGSP & H

N	N	N	N	N
L	L	L	L	L
P	P	P	P	P
G	G	G	G	G
I	I	I	I	I

n	n	n	n	n
l	l	l	l	l
p	p	p	p	p
g	g	g	g	g
i	i	i	i	i

© NGSP & H

R	R	R	R	R
D	D	D	D	D
C	C	C	C	C
V	V	V	V	V
O	O	O	O	O

r	r	r	r	r
d	d	d	d	d
c	c	c	c	c
v	v	v	v	v
o	o	o	o	o

© NGSP & H

J	J	J	J	J
B	B	B	B	B
W	W	W	W	W
K	K	K	K	K
E	E	E	E	E

j j j j j

b b b b b

w w w w w

k k k k k

e e e e e

© NGSP & H

Z	Z	Z	Z	Z
Y	Y	Y	Y	Y
Qu	Qu	Qu	Qu	Qu
X	X	X	X	X
U	U	U	U	U

z z z z z

y y y y y

qu qu qu qu qu

x x x x x

u u u u u

© NGSP & H

Manuscript Alphabet

 Look at the letters. Trace them with a finger.

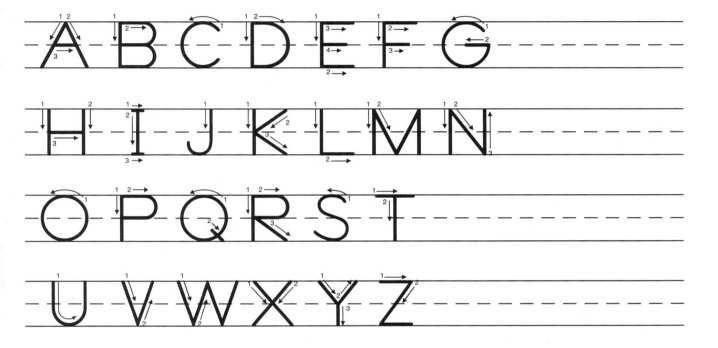

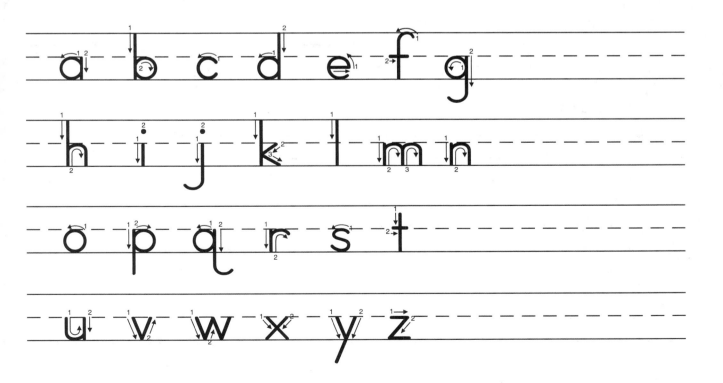

Name _____

Write the letters.

S S S

s s s

M M M

m m m

F F F

f f f

H H H

h h h

T T T

t t t

A A A

a a a

© NGSP &

Name ______________________________

Write the letters.

N N N

n n n

L L L

l l l

P P P

p p p

G G G

g g g

I I I

i i i

Name _____

✐ Write the letters.

R R R

r r r

D D D

d d d

C C C

c c c

V V V

v v v

O O O

o o o

© NGSP &

Name ______________________________

Write the letters.

J J J

j j j

B B B

b b b

W W W

w w w

K K K

k k k

E E E

e e e

Name _____

Write the letters.

Z Z Z

Z Z Z

Y Y Y

y y y

U U U

u u u

Q Q Q

q q q

X X X

X X X

© NGSP &

Yes

School

Not

No

It

Number

Show

Look

Point

Me

The

This

You

Name

My

Is

I

Am

yes   it   point

school   number   me   you   is

not   show   the   name   I

no   look   this   my   am

© NGSP & H

Girl	She	Write		Tomorrow
Boy	He	That	Who	Day
They	Answer	Play	What	At
We	Read	Can	Time	

girl	she	write
boy	he	that	who	tomorrow
they	answer	play	what	day
we	read	can	time	at

© NGSP & H

Both

Does

Do

Book

Picture

How

These

Good

Don't

Those

Like

And

An

A

Are

Of

Some

Food

both

picture

don't

does

how

those

an

of

do

these

like

a

some

book

good

and

are

food

© NGSP & H

Need	With	Them	Group
Help	Little	Your	Things
Too	Very	Put	Feel
Get	Great	Old	
Has	Call	Have	

NGSP & HB

need

with

them

group

help

little

your

things

too

very

put

feel

get

great

old

has

call

have

© NGSP &

Year	Think	Night	For
Soon	Later	See	Which
Will	Here	Letters	To
In	Where	Around	Work
On	Take		Give

year	soon	will		in
think	later	here	where	on
night	see	letters	around	take
for	which	to	work	give

© NGSP &